ANNA
WILKINSON

LEARN TO
CROCHET
love TO
CROCHET

PHOTOGRAPHY BY
LAURA EDWARDS

QUADRILLE

✛CONTENTS

LEARN TO CROCHET PROJECTS

LOVE TO CROCHET PROJECTS

✝INTRODUCTION

I first learned how to crochet ten years ago after watching my mother crocheting. I loved the simplicity and rhythm of crochet, working just one stitch at a time before moving on to the next. While I managed to pick up a very basic stitch simply by observing, I didn't make anything useful for quite a while. Instead I spent time playing around with basic increases and decreases, creating freeform shapes and three-dimensional bags. It felt wonderfully tactile. I had learned to knit at a very young age and so where I was used to knitting in rows and only seeing the shapes produced by increases and decreases after binding off, with crochet I could see what I was creating as I worked, altering the shapes as I went along. With crochet you can make absolutely any shape you can think of, as you are thinking it up.

As with any new technique, at first I found crochet a little awkward. The hand positions used to hold the hook and yarn can feel alien to begin with, especially as you start with a single slip knot and create everything from that one loop. With patience, persistence, and practice, this awkwardness quickly passes and anything becomes possible. There are only a few basic crochet stitches to learn and everything else is a variation on these few stitches. Once you are comfortable holding your hook and yarn, you will be well on your way with your colorful and exciting crochet journey.

The **LEARN TO CROCHET** projects in this book include some basic patterns—a good place to start if you haven't tried crochet before. These projects are small and manageable, designed to enable you to get familiar with the craft and the basic stitches. As you progress through the book the projects build in difficulty, introducing new techniques that will allow you to learn and practice new skills. Once you are comfortable with the basic crochet stitches, move on to the **LOVE TO CROCHET** projects. They may look a little daunting at first glance, but once you have mastered the basic stitches you will be able to make any of these garments. If you have crocheted before, feel free to jump in wherever you like. As some are larger garments or worked in finer yarns, these projects require greater concentration and are more time consuming. Do not panic if you make a mistake—the wonderful thing about crochet is that you'll only be working one stitch at a time so can you easily unravel your work to go back a couple of steps and redo where you went wrong.

As I learned how to knit long before I attempted crochet, I find it difficult to talk about crocheting without mentioning knitting. I am often asked to compare the two. Which do I prefer? Which is better? It's more complicated than that. I can't say I prefer one over the other, but what I have learned through practice is that, despite a few similarities, each craft produces different fabrics that lend themselves to different projects. Crochet is a wonderful and simple technique that, once mastered, can be used to create amazing garments, accessories, and homewares really quickly. It's a very rhythmic craft and when you have the hang of the basic stitches, you'll have all the knowledge you need to make anything you like and then you can start exploring your own individual crochet style.

There is nothing more rewarding than making something by hand. Objects made by machine will never compare to your own creations. Whether it is for you or a loved one, a handmade garment will be cherished. I have loved designing and making every garment and accessory within this book. I hope that you too enjoy making these projects. Whether you are a complete beginner or have been crocheting for years, I hope this book becomes a part of your journey as a crocheter and that it inspires you to continue exploring other patterns, possibilities, and maybe even designing your own projects.

CROCHET BASICS

Unlike other crafts, crochet does not require a vast amount of special equipment. The only tool that is absolutely essential for crochet is the hook, although a handful of other items will improve your work and make crocheting easier and more enjoyable.

CROCHET HOOKS are available in a variety of materials as well as sizes, colors, and designs. Some come with grips for your fingers while others don't. As you practice crochet, you will discover the type of crochet hook that feels most comfortable in your hand. The size of the hook you need will depend on the thickness of the yarn you use. The smallest steel hooks designed for intricate lacework start at US size 14 steel. The most commonly used hooks start at US size D/3 and go up to US size N-P/15, but even larger plastic and wooden ones are available for supersized crochet. The hook's metric size correlates to the diameter measurement taken across the shank—the part of the crochet hook between the tip and throat and the grip. When checking a hook using a size gauge, the shank should fit snugly into the correct size hole. Measurements do vary slightly depending on the manufacturer, so it is always sensible to crochet and measure a gauge swatch (see pages 26–27) before beginning a project to ensure you are using the correct size hook.

IN YOUR BASIC CROCHET WORKBOX YOU WILL ALSO NEED:

BLUNT-TIPPED YARN OR TAPESTRY NEEDLE for stitching pieces together and weaving in loose yarn ends.

PEN AND PAPER for jotting down handy notes on your work as you follow a pattern.

PINS AND SAFETY PINS for pinning pieces together before you sew seams to make sure everything stays in place.

SCISSORS for snipping yarns.

STEAM IRON for finishing and pressing.

STITCH MARKERS are useful for highlighting specific stitches or points in your work. You can use anything from safety pins to snippets of yarn that contrast in color from the main working yarn. Alternatively, you can buy stitch markers that look like plastic safety pins.

TAPE MEASURE for checking gauge and measuring the dimensions of garment pieces when necessary.

HOOK SIZES

US	METRIC	UK IMPERIAL
4 steel	2mm	14
B/1	2.25mm	13
C/2	2.75mm	
	3mm	11
D/3	3.25mm	10
E/4	3.5mm	9
F/5	3.75mm	
G/6	4mm	8
7	4.5mm	7
H/8	5mm	6
I/9	5.5mm	5
J/10	6mm	4
K/10½	6.5mm	3
	7mm	2
L/11	8mm	0
M-N/13	9mm	00
N-P/15	10mm	000

CHOOSING YARNS

Yarns come in a vast range of colors, thicknesses, and textures. There are some amazingly beautiful yarns out there—some of which have been hand dyed in vibrant colors and hand spun using locally sourced fibers. You will see yarns made from animal fibers, such as angora, alpaca, cashmere, and wool, as well as plant fibers, including cotton, linen, hemp, and even bamboo. As you become immersed in the craft of crochet, you will find yourself drawn to certain yarn types and colors. Experimenting with the different yarns available and developing your own crochet style can be a lot of fun. You will find that particular yarns cry out to be made into specific projects and that you must oblige. Other yarns will simply demand to be bought without projects immediately springing to mind. Over time you will get a good sense of what yarns work for which projects, as well as the thicknesses of yarn that you prefer to work with.

At the beginning of every crochet pattern, a recommended yarn is suggested along with the amount of yarn. This is the yarn that the photographed garment or accessory has been made up in. This doesn't mean that you can only use the recommended yarn for that pattern. You can use any yarn that you like as long as the gauge achieved matches the gauge given in the pattern.

Yarns generally come in universal weights or thicknesses, such as lace, fingering, sport, double knitting, worsted, Aran, bulky, and super bulky. The yardage (meterage) and weight of a substitute yarn may differ to that of the yarn used in the pattern, so do be aware if you are using a substitute that you may need to buy more or fewer balls/hanks. Always buy a substitute yarn according to the yardage (meterage) of a ball rather than by its weight. Also be very careful to ensure that your gauge matches that of the pattern when working with a different yarn—you may just need to alter your hook size. The specifications for all the yarns used in this book are given on page 142.

The six categories of yarn weights given in the Craft Council of American guidelines are:
Lace (0): lace, fingering, 10-count crochet thread
Super fine (1): sock, fingering, baby
Fine (2): sport, baby
Light (3): double knitting, light worsted
Medium (4): worsted, afghan, Aran
Bulky (5): chunky, craft, rug
Super bulky (6): bulky, roving

YARN LABELS

Yarn labels carry a lot of information and so it's worth keeping hold of one per project just in case you need to refer back to any of that information, in particular the washing instructions. Usually, yarn labels contain the following:

BRAND NAME This is the name of the yarn manufacturer.

YARN NAME This can be an informative description including the weight of yarn, but it may also be an evocative name.

YARN COMPOSITION This details which fibers the yarn is made up of and the amount of each expressed as a percentage.

SHADE NAME OR NUMBER The color of a yarn is often given as a name—which can be either straightforward or lyrical—but it also usually has a code number.

DYE LOT NUMBER This is an important number to be aware of as it denotes the batch in which the yarn has been dyed. Yarn is generally dyed in large batches and each lot is given its own individual code number that is printed on the yarn label. Often there is little difference between dye lots but sometimes yarn from separate batches can vary in shade. Before starting a project, make sure your yarn is from the same dye lot with identical codes. Ordinarily this isn't a problem as yarn stores and online retailers stock balls or hanks from the same dye lot. If you do run out of yarn midway through a project, you will need to have the dye lot number at hand so that you can request stock from the same batch when ordering more yarn.

WASHING INSTRUCTIONS This is essential information so you do not ruin a project that you have worked really hard on. Always pay close attention to the washing instructions given on a yarn label. If in doubt, hand wash the garment gently in cool water and allow it to dry flat.

RECOMMENDED NEEDLE/HOOK SIZE This gives a suggested knitting needle or crochet hook size for the weight of yarn.

GAUGE This is the ideal number of stitches and rows to a specific area (usually 4in/10cm square) when worked on a particular size crochet hook or knitting needle.

YARDAGE/METERAGE This states how many yards/meters of yarn are contained in an individual ball or hank of yarn.

WEIGHT This states how many grams/ounces of yarn are contained in an individual ball or hank of yarn.

READING PATTERNS

Once you have practiced the basic crochet stitches, the next step is to understand how to work from patterns, learn the common abbreviations used in these patterns, and bring all of these skills together. At first a crochet pattern can seem a little daunting with its apparent jumble of letters and numbers, but once you have taken a good look at the list of standard abbreviations on this page, it will all start to make more sense. Some patterns you encounter may be written out longhand with the terms explained in full, but it is more likely that the crochet patterns you see most often will be written using these abbreviations. It is important to take the time to read carefully through your pattern before you begin work so that you don't miss any important steps.

HOW TO READ A CROCHET PATTERN

The first word of a line of instruction lets you know whether you are working the stitches in a straight row or in a round. The first stitches to work are the beginning chain stitches that set up the row or round. The instructions will also tell you whether or not the chains are to be counted as your first stitch within your overall stitch count. These chains are worked to make sure that the first stitch of the row or round is going to be worked at the same height as the rest of the stitches. Any instructions given inside brackets [ ] indicate that this is to be repeated the number of times given directly after the closing bracket or into the stitch specified. An asterisk means that the instructions that follow are then repeated by the number of times stated or to the end of the row or round. The instruction "join" is usually used when working in the round and means you need to join the first and last stitches in the round with a slip stitch. The stitch counts given (in italics) after a line of instruction tell you how many stitches you should have after working that specific row or round.

HOW TO WORK FROM A CROCHET STITCH DIAGRAM

Crochet patterns often come accompanied by a stitch diagram. At first these can look like assortments of shapes, but when you know what each symbol means, it can be really helpful to work from these diagrams. They provide more of a clear visual guide to what your finished crocheting should look like.

MAIN SYMBOLS

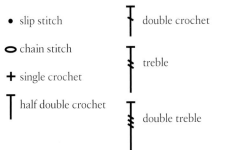

- slip stitch

○ chain stitch

+ single crochet

half double crochet

double crochet

treble

double treble

ABBREVIATIONS

The following list shows the most commonly used abbreviations within crochet patterns. You'll see these shorthand terms popping up a lot, so keep this list handy until you start to get used to these abbreviations.

alt	alternate
beg	begin/beginning
ch	chain(s)
ch sp(s)	chain space(s)
cl	cluster(s)
col	color
cont	continue/continuing
dc	double crochet(s)
dec	decrease(s)/decreasing
dtr	double treble(s)
foll	follow(s)/following
g	gram(s)
gr	group(s)
hdc	half double(s)
inc	increase(s)/increasing
lp(s)	loop(s)
oz	ounce(s)
patt(s)	pattern(s)
rem	remain(s)/remaining
rep(s)	repeat(s)/repeating
rnd(s)	round(s)
RS	right side
sc	single crochet(s)
sp(s)	space(s)
sl st	slip stitch
st(s)	stitch(es)
tch	turning chain
tog	together
tr	treble(s)
trtr	triple treble(s)
WS	wrong side
yo	yarn over (hook)
[ ]	work instructions within brackets as many times as directed
( )	contains additional instruction or further clarification

When working from any crochet pattern, be very aware of whether the instructions are written using US or UK crochet terminology. There is huge potential for confusion if you start working from a British crochet pattern without realizing that some of the stitches are named differently. For example, the stitch known as "treble crochet" in UK terminology is actually the US "double crochet." All of the patterns in this book are written using US crochet terminology.

SLIP KNOT

The starting point of any piece of crochet you make will be a slip knot, which will be your starting stitch. This first stitch will either be the first stitch of a foundation chain when working in rows or the first stitch of a base ring when working in the round. When making a slip knot you only really need to leave a short tail of yarn at least 4in (10cm) long, which will be just long enough to stitch in the yarn end easily once you have finished crocheting.

STEP 1 Leaving a yarn tail at least 4in (10cm) long, curl the yarn into a loop.

STEP 2 With your crochet hook, enter the loop you have created and catch the working end of the yarn (the end attached to the ball of yarn) and pull it through the center of the loop. Pull gently on both ends of the yarn to tighten. You may now continue to make your foundation chain or base ring as per the pattern instructions you are following.

HOLDING THE HOOK AND YARN

Holding a crochet hook may feel strange at first and take a little practice before it feels comfortable, but with persistence you will soon be whizzing through patterns. As you learn to crochet, take the time to get the basic techniques right to ensure an even gauge. One hand holds the crochet hook, as though holding a pen or pencil. The other hand holds the working yarn and plays the role of feeding the hook with yarn, thereby determining the gauge. There are two methods shown here for holding the yarn; try both to see which you prefer. The technique is the same whether you are left- or right-handed.

METHOD ONE Wrap the working yarn around your little finger, across your two middle fingers, behind your index finger, and to the front to rest on your elevated index finger. There should be approximately 4in (10cm) between your index finger and the loop on your hook.

METHOD TWO Use this method if you find it more comfortable. Lay the working yarn across your palm and under your index finger, then wrap it twice around your index finger. There should be about 4in (10cm) between your index finger and the loop on your hook.

MAKING CHAIN STITCHES

The beginning of any crocheted fabric is usually a length of chain stitches, so the chain stitch will be the first stitch that you learn and practice. It is important to keep your chain stitches even, neither too tight nor too loose, so that they are easy to insert the hook into when you work your first row or round. (Chains are also used at the ends of rows in order to take the hook up to the correct height before you start working on the next row. This is called a turning chain and it is explained on page 13.)

STEP 1 With the slip knot sitting on the neck of your hook, hold the working yarn keeping a good tension on the tail end. Pass the hook from left to right under the working yarn, and around the yarn in a counterclockwise movement, to catch the yarn in the crook of the hook. This is called "yarn over" hook (abbreviated yo).

STEP 2 Draw the working yarn through the slip knot or the stitch already on the hook. Keep the yarn under tension at all times. As you draw the working yarn through your loop, rotate the hook so that the crook is facing downward. You have now made one new chain (ch). Repeat these two steps to create more chain stitches. To maintain a good tension on the yarn, you will need to reposition the fingers holding the yarn every four or five stitches.

COUNTING CHAINS

When counting chains, do not include the stitch or loop that is sitting on the hook. This is because a loop always remains on the hook right up to the point that you fasten off your work. To make it easier to count chains when counting a large number, it is a good idea to place stitch markers at intervals, such as after every 10 or 20 stitches. Whenever possible, stitches should be counted from the front of the chain.

THE FRONT OF A CHAIN
The front of the chain will look like a series of V shapes. Each V is a chain loop sitting between two other chain loops. The first chain made will have the slip knot sitting directly before it. The surface of the chain is smooth on this front side.

THE REVERSE OF A CHAIN
The reverse of the chain has a row of bumps that sit behind the V-shapes and run in a straight line from the slip knot to the hook. The surface of the reverse of the chain is more textural than the front side.

⁺WORKING SINGLE CROCHET

FIRST ROW

Working the first row of a crochet fabric can be difficult as you will be working into each of the chains you have just worked on the foundation chain. Depending on which crochet stitch you are working in, you will be instructed to skip a number of chains from the hook. The skipped chains take your hook up to the correct height from the chain according to the stitch you are working in. Here we are working in single crochet (sc) so the first stitch is worked into the second chain from the hook.

STEP 1 Insert the hook into the second chain from the hook, into the center of the V-shape. (The number of chains skipped changes according to the crochet stitch being worked.) You can place your hook into the top side of the chain, thus working over just one strand, or the lower part of the chain, thus working over two strands. Working into the top side of the chain is the easiest method for a beginner, though it does result in a looser edge.

STEP 2 Wrap your working yarn from back to front over the hook. This is called "yarn over" (yo).

STEP 3 Catch the working yarn with your hook and draw it through the chain to the front of your work.

STEP 4 Wrap your working yarn from back to front over the hook again.

STEP 5 Draw the yarn through both loops on the hook. One single crochet has been completed. Repeat these steps to the end of the foundation chain.

TURNING CHAINS

When you reach the end of any row and turn your work ready to begin the next row, you need to create a turning chain (tch) to bring your hook up to the correct height for the stitch to be worked along this row. Likewise, turning chains are usually used when working in rounds.

The number of chains needed in a turning chain depends on the crochet stitch being first worked in that row or round. If your next stitch is a single crochet (sc), your turning chain needs to be one chain. If you are working in half double crochet (hdc), your turning chain will be two chains. If you are working in double crochet (dc), your turning chain will be three chains.

Making a turning chain is very simple. Create the number of chains you need by wrapping the working yarn around the hook (yo) and drawing this yarn through the loop already on the hook. This counts as one chain. Repeat to make the requisite number of chains according to which stitch you are working in.

Unless otherwise stated, your turning chain is not counted as part of the overall stitch count, and the first stitch of a new row is worked into the first stitch in the row below (the stitch at the base of the turning chain). If the turning chain is counted as the first stitch of the row, the first stitch of the row below is skipped and the next stitch is worked into the second stitch in the row below; then at the end of the row the final stitch is worked into the top of the turning chain in the row below.

FOLLOWING ROWS OF SINGLE CROCHET

STEP 1 You will see that a row of Vs run along the top edge of your crochet. Once you have worked your turning chain, insert your hook under the next V along.

STEP 2 As with the first row, wrap the working yarn around the hook (yo) and draw this yarn through the V so that you now have two loops sitting on your hook.

STEP 3 Wrap the working yarn around the hook again and draw it through both of the two loops on your hook. One single crochet has been completed. Repeat these steps to the end of the row.

⁺WORKING DOUBLE CROCHET

Double crochet (dc) is a longer stitch than single crochet (sc), so it forms a more open and therefore less dense fabric. As each individual stitch is longer, when working in double crochet the fabric grows quickly. When working lacy stitch patterns, double crochet is often used as the main stitch in combination with chains.

STEP 1 Work a foundation chain consisting of the specified number of chains plus an additional three chains for the turning chain. As the turning chain is made up of three chains for double crochet, the first stitch is worked into the fourth chain from the hook. Begin the first double by wrapping the working yarn around the hook.

STEP 2 Insert your hook into the fourth chain from the hook if working your first row or into the next stitch (V) along if working your second row or any subsequent row.

STEP 3 Pass the hook from left to right, or counterclockwise, under the working yarn to catch the yarn in the hook again.

STEP 4 Draw the yarn through the chain (or stitch) so there are now three loops sitting on your hook.

STEP 5 Wrap the working yarn around the hook again, as in step 3.

STEP 6 Draw the yarn through the first two loops on the hook, so there are now two loops sitting on your hook.

STEP 7 Wrap the working yarn around the hook again and draw it through the remaining two loops on the hook.

STEP 8 One double crochet has been completed. Repeat these steps to the end of the row, beginning by wrapping the yarn around the hook and inserting it into the next foundation chain (or next stitch along) as in step 2.

WORKING HALF DOUBLE CROCHET

STEP 1 Work a foundation chain consisting of the specified number of chains plus an additional two chains for the turning chain. As the turning chain is made up of two chains for half double crochet, the first stitch is worked into the third chain from the hook. Begin the first half double by wrapping the working yarn around the hook.

STEP 2 Insert your hook into the third chain from the hook if working your first row or into the next stitch (V) along if working your second row or any subsequent row.

STEP 3 Pass the hook from left to right, or counterclockwise, under the working yarn to catch the yarn in the hook again.

STEP 4 Draw the yarn through the chain (or stitch) so there are now three loops sitting on your hook.

STEP 5 Wrap the working yarn around the hook again, as in step 3.

STEP 6 Draw the yarn through all three loops on the hook. One half double has been completed. Repeat these steps to the end of the row, beginning by wrapping the yarn around the hook and inserting it into the next foundation chain (or next stitch along) as in step 2.

FASTENING OFF

It is very easy to fasten off a piece of crochet. Once you have completed your final stitch you will have just one loop remaining on the hook. Snip the working yarn leaving a tail at least 4in (10cm) long. Using your fingers, loosen the loop of the final stitch and carefully remove it from the hook. Pass the tail of yarn through this final stitch loop and gently pull the tail end to close the loop and secure the stitch.

SLIP STITCH

//

When you work in the round you will often start with a foundation chain that is then joined by a slip stitch (sl st) to form the foundation ring.

STEP 1 To join your foundation chain into a ring, insert the hook from the front to the back into the first chain made.

STEP 2 Wrap the working yarn around the hook.

FIRST ROUND

STEP 3 Draw the working yarn through both the chain and the loop on the hook to complete the slip stitch.

STEP 4 You will now have one loop on the hook and the foundation ring has been formed. Work one chain before you begin the next round; this chain counts as your first stitch. The number of chains you make will depend on the stitch you are working in.

STEP 1 Insert the hook from front to back into the center space of the foundation ring. Wrap the working yarn around the hook.

STEP 2 Draw the yarn through so you have two loops sitting on your hook. Wrap the working yarn around the hook once more.

STEP 3 Draw the yarn through both loops sitting on your hook. There is now one loop on the hook and one single crochet stitch has been made.

STEP 4 Repeat steps 1–3 until the required number of stitches have been worked into the center of the foundation ring.

STEP 5 To join the first round together with a slip stitch, insert your hook into the first stitch of the round.

STEP 6 Wrap the working yarn around the hook.

STEP 7 Draw the yarn through the stitch and the loop already on the hook to complete the slip stitch. One full round has been completed.

⊹INCREASING STITCHES

INCREASING IN THE ROUND

When working in the round, to produce a nice flat circle you need to increase (inc) at certain points. Increasing is really simple and just means that you are increasing the number of stitches in each round, making the circumference larger.

STEP 1 Make your turning chain at the beginning of the round—here we are working the round in double crochet so three chains have been worked for the turning chain. Work your first double crochet into the next stitch along. Wrap the working yarn around the hook in preparation for the next double.

STEP 2 To increase by one stitch, you simply need to work two stitches into the same stitch. So, insert your hook back into the same stitch that you have just worked into.

INCREASING IN ROWS

Increasing stitches (inc) when working in rows of crochet uses exactly the same method as increasing while working in the round. You simply work two or more crochet stitches into a single stitch in the row below.

STEP 3 Wrap the working yarn around the hook, draw the yarn through to the front of the work.

STEP 4 Complete the double crochet in the usual way. You will see that you have increased by working two stitches into one stitch in the row below.

SINGLE CROCHET DECREASE

Decreasing (dec) by one stitch at a time is really simple and decreases are usually made by working two stitches together. The decreasing method changes slightly depending on which crochet stitch you are working in. The method shown below is working two single crochets together to make one stitch from two. The abbreviation for this is sc2tog.

STEP 1 To decrease, insert your hook into the next stitch, wrap the working yarn around the hook and draw the loop through. You now have two loops on your hook.

STEP 2 Instead of wrapping the yarn around the hook and drawing it through the remaining loops to finish the single crochet, insert your hook into the next stitch, wrap the yarn around the hook and draw through the stitch so that you have three loops sitting on your hook.

STEP 3 Wrap the working yarn around the hook once more and draw the yarn through all three of the loops on your hook. One single crochet has now been decreased.

⁺HALF DOUBLE DECREASE

A half double decrease to create one stitch from two stitches is worked in a similar way to the single crochet decrease, in that you work half the stitch, then move on to the next stitch before drawing them both together to form one stitch. The abbreviation for this decrease is hdc2tog.

STEP 1 To decrease when working in half double crochet (hdc), wrap the working yarn around the hook (called "yarn over" ore "yo"), insert the hook into the next stitch, yarn over (yo) again and then draw the yarn through the stitch so you have three loops sitting on your hook.

STEP 2 Instead of continuing and finishing the half double as you usually would, wrap the yarn around the hook again and insert your hook into the next stitch along.

STEP 3 Wrap the yarn a round the hook again and draw the yarn through the stitch so there are now five loops sitting on your hook.

STEP 4 Yarn over (yo) once more, then draw the yarn all the way through all the five loops sitting on your hook. You have now completed your decrease and one half double crochet stitch has been decreased.

DOUBLE CROCHET DECREASE

STEP 1 Wrap the working yarn around the hook (called "yarn over" ore "yo"), insert the hook into the next stitch, yarn over (yo) once more and draw the yarn through to the front of the work so that you now have three loops on your hook.

STEP 2 Wrap the yarn around the hook again then draw the yarn through the first two loops on your hook.

STEP 3 There are now two loops on your hook.

STEP 4 Wrap the yarn around your hook again and insert your hook into the next stitch along.

STEP 5 Yarn over (yo) again and draw yarn through to the front of your work so you now have four loops sitting on your crochet hook. Yarn over (yo) again and then draw the yarn through the first two loops on your hook.

STEP 6 You now have three loops on your crochet hook. Lastly, yarn over (yo) once more and draw the yarn through all three remaining loops on your hook to complete your decrease. One double crochet has been decreased. The abbreviation for this is dc2tog.

⁺STEP DECREASE

Most of the time, when you're crocheting, you will find that most decreases (decs) are made gradually—by turning two stitches into one. However, you will occasionally need to decrease abruptly in steps at the side edge of your work, when working armhole shaping for example. You will only need to work this step decrease at the beginning of a row, because if you need to decrease in a step at the end of a row, you simply stop the row early by however many stitches you require and turn, shortening your row.

STEP 1 Begin your row by slip stitching along the number of stitches required to make your step decrease. First make one chain. Then to work each slip stitch, simply insert the hook through the next stitch, yarn over (yo) and draw a loop through the stitch and the loop on the hook. Slip stitches are the shortest crochet stitches so this makes them ideal for moving across a row without your work growing in height.

STEP 2 When you have completed your slip stitches, you will then need to make a turning chain to bring your hook up to the correct height. The number of chains will depend on which crochet stitch you're working in.

STEP 3 Work your next stitch as normal in your crochet stitch pattern.

STEP 4 Continue to the end of the row. You will be able to see your step decrease at the beginning of your row.

JOINING IN A NEW COLOR

IN THE MIDDLE OF A ROW

STEP 1 The method for changing color is the same whether you're working in rows or rounds. You need to plan ahead slightly as you begin your color change the stitch before. When working the final stitch before your color change, stop before the final yarn over (yo). Cut off the old color yarn, leaving a long tail. Leaving a long tail, loop your new color yarn around your hook.

STEP 2 Draw the new color yarn through the remaining loops on your hook to finish off the stitch. Gently pull the old and new color yarn ends to tighten the loop on the hook. Changing color will create yarn ends which you can either weave into the back of your work afterward or you can work over them with your crocheting of the next few stitches to fasten them in place.

STEP 3 Now that you have fastened in your new color, continue to work the rest of the row in the new color yarn according to the pattern instructions that you are following.

AT THE END OF A ROW

STEP 1 Changing color at the end of a row is similar to changing color in the middle of row as you must plan ahead. Before you work the final yarn over (yo) of the final stitch of the row, cut off your old color leaving a long tail and loop your new color yarn around the hook.

STEP 2 Draw your new color yarn through the remaining two loops on your hook to finish off the final stitch of that row. Gently pull the old and new color yarn ends to tighten the loop on the hook.

VSTEP 3 Continue to work in your crochet pattern, beginning with your turning chain to start the next row. Then, just work the rest of the row in your new color according to your pattern instructions.

+MATTRESS STITCH

Mattress stitch is a great stitch to learn as it leaves you with really neat seams that are almost unnoticeable. What I really love about mattress stitch is that it is worked with the right sides of the fabric facing toward you, so as you stitch you can keep an eye on how your work will look on the outside.

To work mattress stitch, lay the two pieces of crochet that you would like to sew together on a flat surface with the right sides facing upward. With a tapestry needle, begin by stitching down into the fabric on the right-hand side, close to the seam edge. Then stitch upward into the fabric on the left-hand side, and down into this fabric a short distance above, upward into the fabric on the right-hand side, down into this fabric again a short distance above. Repeat this for a few stitches and then gently pull each end of the yarn that you're working with to tighten up your seam. Continue to work like this along the full length of the seam and then weave in the ends of the yarn into the back of your work.

Making gauge swatches can seem painstaking to begin with, but they're incredibly important, especially if you are a beginner crocheter. There might be a few projects that you can get away with jumping head first into without doing a gauge swatch, such as accessories, or if you're working on a homewares project, any projects where the measurements don't need to be strictly precise.

If you're making a garment, however, definitely force yourself to make a gauge swatch first. This way you can ensure that your gauge matches the gauge of the pattern and therefore you will be able to make your garment to the precise size that you would like and it will fit you properly. As you become a more experienced crocheter you will get an idea of what your gauge is usually like and whether you need to go up or down a hook size to reach the required gauge. You'll get quicker working up gauge swatches and matching the gauge given in the pattern.

The gauge given at the beginning of a crochet pattern is usually written by giving the number of stitches and rows in a 4in (10cm) square. If a project is to be crocheted up in a bulky yarn, then the gauge may be given over a larger area just so it's more of a precise measurement. It's best to crochet a slightly bigger square than 4in (10cm), by an inch (2.5cm) extra, so that you can take your gauge measurement from the center of your swatch.

When you have crocheted a good-sized swatch, lay it out on a flat surface. Take a tape measure and use pins to mark out a 4in (10cm) square, then count the stitches and rows within this square. Once you have counted your stitches and rows you can compare your gauge to that given in the pattern.

If your gauge matches that given at the beginning of the pattern, then that's great! Your garment will crochet up to the exact size required. If your gauge doesn't match, don't worry. If you find that you have more stitches within the 4in (10cm) than the pattern states, this means that your gauge is too tight so try working another gauge swatch using a slightly thicker crochet hook. If you find that you have fewer stitches within the 4in (10cm), then this means that your gauge is to loose so try working another gauge swatch using a slightly thinner hook. It may seem a little painstaking, but it's definitely worth getting right.

CHECKING GAUGE

✝BUTTONHOLES

HORIZONTAL

STEP 1 Buttonholes usually sit a few stitches in from the edge of the garment. Work your stitch until you reach the point you'd like to position your buttonhole, then work the number of chains to correspond with the size of the button. Make sure the buttonhole is slightly smaller than the button so that the fastening stays firmly closed.

STEP 2 Skip the same number of stitches as the number of chains you have just made, then work into the next stitch as usual. This chain bridges the gap over your skipped stitches and you have created a buttonhole.

STEP 3 Crochet to the end of the row as usual. When you work the next row, work until you reach the chain-space, crochet the same number of stitches into the chain space as were skipped. As this stage, test the hole with your button—it should go through relatively easily but not too loosely. If the hole isn't right, rework.

VERTICAL

STEP 1 Vertical buttonholes are worked by dividing the piece of crochet into two sections at the position of the buttonhole and working the same number of rows on each side. You then join up the two sides afterward. To begin, work in your stitch pattern to the point you would like to make a buttonhole, turn and work on these stitches on this side of your buttonhole until you have worked the length you would like your buttonhole.

STEP 2 Cut off your yarn, skip one stitch at the point of your buttonhole, then rejoin your yarn and work to the end of the row. Work just on these stitches on this side of the buttonhole until you have worked the same number of rows as on the other side of the buttonhole. Work up to the point of the buttonhole, work one chain, and then join to the other side by continuing to work along those stitches to the end of the row.

STEP 3 When working the next row, when you reach the chain-space you've just created at the buttonhole, crochet one stitch into the chain space to make up for the stitch you skipped in the row below. Test the hole with your button to ensure that the size is correct. You want your button to go through relatively easily but not to slide through.

+LEARN TO
CROCHET

⁺SIMPLE WRISTWARMERS

//

YOU WILL NEED

YARN

For one pair of plain wristwarmers

2 x 25g (⅞oz) balls of Jamieson's of Shetland *Spindrift*, or a similar super-fine-weight wool yarn, in one color, such as mustard (1160 Scotch Broom)

For one pair of striped wristwarmers

1 x 25g (⅞oz) ball of Jamieson's of Shetland *Spindrift* and 1 x 50g (1¾oz) of JC Rennie *Supersoft Lambswool 4ply*, or a similar super-fine-weight wool yarn, in each of four colors:

A *Spindrift* in green-blue (769 Willow)
B *Spindrift* in charcoal (109 Black/Shaela)
C *Spindrift* in pale pink (268 Dog Rose)
D *Supersoft Lambswool 4ply* in dark red (380 Blaze)

For one pair of blue and mustard wristwarmers

1 x 25g (⅞oz) ball of Jamieson's of Shetland *Spindrift* and 1 x 50g (1¾oz) of JC Rennie *Supersoft Lambswool 4ply*, or a similar super-fine-weight wool yarn, in each of four colors:

A *Spindrift* in charcoal (109 Black/Shaela)
B *Spindrift* in mustard (1160 Scotch Broom)
C *Spindrift* in medium blue (136 Teviot)
D *Supersoft Lambswool 4ply* in dark red (380 Blaze)

CROCHET HOOKS

US sizes G/6 and H/8 (4mm and 5mm) crochet hooks

OTHER EQUIPMENT

Blunt-tipped yarn or tapestry needle, for weaving in yarn ends and sewing seams

GAUGE

18 sts and 20 rows to 4in (10cm) measured over half double crochet using a US size G/6 (4mm) crochet hook.

ABBREVIATIONS

See page 9.

SPECIAL ABBREVIATION

hdc2tog = [yo, insert hook in next st, yo and draw a loop through] twice (5 loops now on hook), yo and draw through all 5 loops on hook to decrease one stitch (see page 22).

TWO SIZES

Plain wristwarmers and striped wristwarmers: small–medium

Blue and mustard wristwarmers: large

On the diagram at right the measurements for the smaller size come first and the measurements for the larger size follow in parentheses. Note that the larger size (the blue and mustard wristwarmers) does not have thumbs.

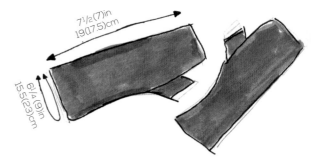

7½(7)in 19(17.5)cm

6¼(9)in 15.5(23)cm

blue and mustard wristwarmers

PLAIN WRISTWARMERS (MAKE 2 ALIKE)

These wristwarmers are worked in one size only—small–medium.

Foundation chain: Using a US size H/8 (5mm) crochet hook, ch 34.

Change to a US size G/6 (4mm) hook and cont working in rows, turning at end of each row.

Row 1: 1 hdc in third ch from hook, 1 hdc in each of next 5 ch, *hdc2tog over next 2 ch, 1 hdc in next 6 ch; rep from * to last 2 ch, hdc2tog over last 2 ch. *28 hdc.*

Row 2: Ch 2 (does NOT count as a st), 1 hdc in each of first 4 hdc, *hdc2tog, 1 hdc in next 5 hdc; rep from * to last 3 hdc, 1 hdc in next hdc, hdc2tog over last 2 hdc. *24 hdc.*

Rows 3–5: Ch 2, 1 hdc in each hdc to end of row.

Rows 6–7: Ch 2, inc 1 st at beg of row by working 2 hdc in first hdc, 1 hdc in each hdc to end of row. *26 hdc.*

Rows 8–12: Ch 2, 1 hdc in each hdc to end of row.

Rows 13–16: Ch 2, inc 1 st at beg of row by working 2 hdc in first hdc, 1 hdc in each hdc to end of row. *30 hdc.*

Cont working in rows, but at the same time place markers on Rows 20 and 27 to indicate position of thumbholes when sewing seam.

Rows 17–28: Ch 2, 1 hdc in each hdc to end of row.

Row 29: Ch 2, hdc2tog, 1 hdc in each hdc to end of row. *29 hdc.*

Rows 30–33: Ch 2, 1 hdc in each hdc to end of row.

Row 34: Ch 2, hdc2tog, 1 hdc in each hdc to end of row. *28 hdc.*

Rows 35–36: Ch 2, 1 hdc in each hdc to end of row.

Row 37: Ch 2, hdc2tog, 1 hdc in each hdc to end of row. *27 hdc.*

Fasten off.

TO FINISH PLAIN WRISTWARMERS

Weave any loose yarn ends into the back of your work so they are not visible from the right side.

Lightly steam both pieces.

Sew the sides of the wristwarmer together to form a tube, leaving an opening between the markers placed at Rows 20 and 27 for the thumbholes.

WORK THE THUMBS

With RS facing and using a US size H/8 (5mm) crochet hook, join yarn to edge at center top of each thumbhole, ch 2 (counts as first hdc), work 10 hdc evenly along each side of wristwarmer around thumbhole (counting 2-ch as a st), ending back at center top, join with a sl st in top of 2-ch. *20 sts.*

Cont to work in rounds, with RS always facing.

Round 1 (RS): Ch 2 (counts as first hdc), 1 hdc in each of next 7 hdc, [hdc2tog] twice, 1 hdc in each of next 8 hdc, join with a sl st in top of 2-ch. *18 sts.*

Round 2: Ch 2, 1 hdc in each of next 6 hdc, [hdc2tog] twice, 1 hdc in each of next 7 hdc, join with a sl st in top of 2-ch. *16 sts.*

Round 3: Ch 2, 1 hdc in each of next 5 hdc, [hdc2tog] twice, 1 hdc in each of next 6 hdc, join with a sl st in top of 2-ch. *14 sts.*

Round 4: Ch 2, 1 hdc in each of next 4 hdc, [hdc2tog] twice, 1 hdc in each of next 5 hdc, join with a sl st in top of 2-ch. *12 sts.*

Round 5: Ch 2, 1 hdc in each of next 3 hdc, [hdc2tog] twice, 1 hdc in each of next 4 hdc, join with a sl st in top of 2-ch. *10 sts.*

Fasten off. Weave in any loose yarn ends.

STRIPED WRISTWARMERS

Work as given for the pair of plain wristwarmers but using the following stripe pattern:

STRIPES FOR FIRST WRISTWARMER

Foundation chain and Rows 1–5: Col C.
Rows 6–7: Col B.
Rows 8–10: Col C.
Rows 11–17: Col A.
Rows 18–19: Col B.
Rows 20–22: Col C.
Row 23: Col D.
Rows 24–25: Col C.
Row 26: Col D.
Rows 27–30: Col A.
Rows 31–35: Col B.
Row 36: Col C.
Row 37: Col D.
Work thumb in Col D.

STRIPES FOR SECOND WRISTWARMER
Foundation chain and Rows 1–9: Col A.
Rows 10–11: Col B.
Rows 12–16: Col C.
Row 17: Col B.
Row 18: Col C.
Rows 19–20: Col D.
Row 21: Col A.
Rows 22–24: Col B.
Rows 25–29: Col C.
Rows 30– 32: Col D.
Rows 33–35: Col A.
Row 36: Col B.
Row 37: Col A.
Work thumb in Col A until end of Round 3.
Work thumb Rounds 4–5 in Col B.

BLUE AND MUSTARD WRISTWARMERS

These wristwarmers are worked in one size only—large.
Both wristwarmers are made using the same stitch
pattern, but following different stripe patterns as follows:

STRIPES FOR FIRST WRISTWARMER
Foundation chain and Rows 1–4: Col A.
Rows 5–15: Col C.
Row 16: Col D.
Rows 17–19: Col C.
Rows 20–21: Col A.
Rows 22–28: Col B.
Rows 29–30: Col A.
Rows 31–35: Col C.

STRIPES FOR SECOND WRISTWARMER
Foundation chain and Rows 1–17: Col B.
Rows 18–19: Col A.

Rows 20–23: Col C.
Rows 24–25: Col A.
Rows 26–27: Col D.
Row 28: Col C.
Rows 29–35: Col B.

TO MAKE WRISTWARMERS
Using a US size H/8 (5mm) crochet hook, ch 43.
Change to a US size G/6 (4mm) hook and cont working
in rows, turning at end of each row.
Row 1: 1 hdc in third ch from hook, 1 hdc in each ch to
end. *41 hdc.*
Row 2: Ch 2 (does NOT count as a st), 1 hdc in each of
first 7 hdc, *hdc2tog, 1 hdc in next 6 hdc; rep from * to
last 2 hdc, hdc2tog over last 2 hdc. *36 hdc.*
Row 3: Ch 2, 1 hdc in each hdc to end of row.
Row 4: Ch 2, 1 hdc in each of first 6 hdc, hdc2tog,
*1 hdc in each of next 10 hdc, hdc2tog; rep from *to last
6 hdc, ending with 1 hdc in each of last 6 hdc. *33 hdc.*
Rows 5–12: Ch 2, 1 hdc in each hdc to end of row.
Rows 13–21: Ch 2, 2 hdc in first hdc, 1 hdc in each hdc
to end of row. *42 hdc.*
Rows 22–29: Ch 2, 1 hdc in each hdc to end of row.
Rows 30–35: Ch 2, hdc2tog, 1 hdc in each hdc to end of
row. *36 sts.*
Fasten off.

TO FINISH BLUE AND MUSTARD WRISTWARMERS

Weave any loose yarn ends into the back of your work so
they are not visible from the right side.
Lightly steam both pieces.
Sew the sides of the wristwarmer together to form a
tube, leaving an opening 1½in (4cm) from the top edge
approximately 1½in (4cm) long for the thumbholes.

SNOOD AND HEADBAND

YOU WILL NEED

YARN

2 x 50g (1¾oz) balls of Orkney Angora *St Magnus DK*, or a similar double-knitting-weight wool yarn, in one color:
A bright red (Scarlet)
1 x 50g (1¾oz) ball of Orkney Angora *St Magnus DK*, or a similar double-knitting-weight wool yarn, in each of two colors:
B mustard (Magical Goose)
C pale blue (Aqua)

CROCHET HOOK
US size G/6 (4mm) crochet hook

OTHER EQUIPMENT
Blunt-tipped yarn or tapestry needle, for weaving in yarn ends and sewing seams

GAUGE
7½ cluster repeats and 16 rows to 4in (10cm) measured over stitch pattern using a US size G/6 (4mm) crochet hook.

ABBREVIATIONS
See page 9.

SNOOD

Foundation chain: Using a US size G/6 (4mm) crochet hook and Col A, ch 125.
Cont working in rows, turning at end of each row.
Row 1: 1 sc in second ch from hook, 1 sc in each ch to end of row. *124 sc.*
Row 2: Change to Col C, ch 1 (does NOT count as a st), 1 sc in first sc, *ch 2, skip 2 sc, 1 sc in next sc; rep from * to end of row.
Row 3: Change to Col A, ch 3 (counts as first dc), 1 dc in first sc, *skip 2 ch, 3 dc in next sc; rep from * to end of row, ending last rep with 2 dc in last sc instead of 3.
Row 4: Still using Col A, ch 1, 1 sc in first dc, *ch 2, skip 2 dc, 1 sc in next dc; rep from * to end of row, working last sc of last rep in top of 3-ch.
Row 5: Change to Col B, work as Row 3.
Row 6: Change to Col A, work as Row 4.
Row 7: Still using Col A, work as Row 3.
Row 8: Change to Col C, work as Row 4.
Row 9: Change to Col A, work as Row 3.
Row 10: Change to Col C, work as Row 4.
Row 11: Change to Col B, work as Row 3.

Row 12: Change to Col C, work as Row 4.
Row 13: Change to Col A, work as Row 3.
Row 14: Change to Col C, work as Row 4.
Row 15: Change to Col A, work as Row 3.
Row 16: Still using Col A, work as Row 4.
Row 17: Change to Col B, work as Row 3.
Row 18: Change to Col A, work as Row 4.
Row 19: Still using A, work as Row 3.
Row 20: Change to Col C, work as Row 4.
Row 21: Change to Col A, work as Row 3.
Row 22: Change to Col C, work as Row 4.
Row 23: Change to Col B, work as Row 3.
Row 24: Change to Col C, work as Row 4.
Row 25: Change to Col A, work as Row 3.
Row 26: Change to Col C, work as Row 4.
Row 27: Change to Col A , work as Row 3.
Row 28: Still using Col A, work as Row 4.
Row 29: Change to Col B, work as Row 3.
Row 30: Change to Col A, work as Row 4.
Row 31: Still using Col A, work as Row 3.
Row 32: Change to Col C, work as Row 4.
Row 33: Change to Col A, work as Row 3.
Fasten off.

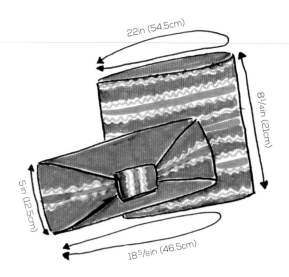

22in (54.5cm)

8¼in (21cm)

5in (12.5cm)

18⅝in (46.5cm)

MAIN HEADBAND

Foundation chain: Using a US size G/6 (4mm) crochet hook and Col A, ch 107.

Cont working in rows, turning at end of each row.

Row 1: 1 sc in second ch from hook, 1 sc in each ch to end of row. *106 sc.*

Row 2: Ch 1 (does NOT count as a st), 1 sc in first sc, *ch 2, skip 2 sc, 1 sc in next sc; rep from * to end of row.

Row 3: Ch 3 (counts as first dc), 1 dc in first sc, *skip 2 ch, 3 dc in next sc; rep from * to end of row, ending last rep with 2 dc in last sc instead of 3.

Row 4: Ch 1, 1 sc in first dc, *ch 2, skip 2 dc, 1 sc in next dc; rep from * to end of row, working last sc of last rep in top of 3-ch.

Row 5: Change to Col B, work as Row 3.

Row 6: Change to Col A, work as Row 4.

Row 7: Still using Col A, work as Row 3.

Row 8: Change to Col C, work as Row 4.

Row 9: Change to Col A, work as Row 3.

Row 10: Change to Col C, work as Row 4.

Row 11: Change to Col B, work as Row 3.

Row 12: Change to Col C, work as Row 4.

Row 13: Change to Col A, work as Row 3.

Row 14: Change to Col C, work as Row 4.

Row 15: Change to Col A, work as Row 3.

Row 16: Still using Col A, work as Row 4.

Row 17: Change to Col B, work as Row 3.

Row 18: Change to Col A, work as Row 4.

Row 19: Still using Col A, work as Row 3.

Row 20: Still using Col A, work as Row 4.

Fasten off.

SMALLER BAND

Foundation chain: Using a US size G/6 (4mm) crochet hook and Col A, ch 26.

Cont working in rows, turning at end of each row.

Row 1: 1 sc in second ch from hook, 1 sc in each ch to end of row. *25 sc.*

Row 2: Ch 1 (does NOT count as a st), 1 sc in first sc, *ch 2, skip 2 sc, 1 sc in next sc; rep from * to end of row.

Row 3: Ch 3 (counts as first dc), 1 dc in first sc, *skip 2 ch, 3 dc in next sc; rep from * to end of row, ending last rep with 2 dc in last sc instead of 3.

Row 4: Change to Col C, ch 1, 1 sc in first dc, *ch 2, skip 2 dc, 1 sc in next dc; rep from * to end of row, working last sc of last rep in top of 3-ch.

Row 5: Change to Col A, work as Row 3.

Row 6: Change to Col C, work as Row 4.

Row 7: Change to Col B, work as Row 3.

Row 8: Change to Col C, work as Row 4.

Row 9: Change to Col A, work as Row 3.

Row 10: Change to Col C, work as Row 4.

Row 11: Change to Col A, work as Row 3.

Row 12: Still using Col A, work as Row 4.

Fasten off.

TO FINISH

Weave any loose yarn ends into the back of your work so they are not visible from the right side.

Lightly steam all the pieces.

Stitch the two short sides of the snood together to form a loop. Sew the main band seam in the same way. Next stitch the smaller band together in the same way, but encasing the main band to hide the main band seam.

+BULL'S-EYE CLUTCH BAGS

//

YOU WILL NEED

YARN

Colorway A

1 x 50g (1¾oz) ball of Rico Design *Creative Cotton Aran*, or a similar Aran-weight wool yarn, in each of three colors:

A pale orange (76 Tangerine)
B dark blue (38 Dark Blue)
C off-white (60 Natural)

Colorway B

1 x 50g (1¾oz) ball of Rico Design *Creative Cotton Aran*, or a similar Aran-weight wool yarn, in each of four colors:

A pale orange (76 Tangerine)
B orange (74 Orange)
C bright pink (13 Fuchsia)
D purple (11 Cardinal)

Colorway C

1 x 50g (1¾oz) ball of Rico Design *Creative Cotton Aran*, or a similar Aran-weight wool yarn, in each of two colors:

A orange (74 Orange)
B bright blue (39 Royal)

Only a small amount of each color yarn is required for one bag, so to make all three clutch bags only one 50g (1¾oz) ball of each of the separate colors is needed.

OTHER MATERIALS

7in (18cm) zipper, for each bag
Lining fabric (optional)
Sewing thread in a matching color, for stitching lining (optional) and zipper into bag

CROCHET HOOK

US size 7 (4.5mm) crochet hook

OTHER EQUIPMENT

Blunt-tipped yarn or tapestry needle, for stitching together bag
Sewing needle, for stitching the lining (optional) and zipper into bag

GAUGE

9–10 sts and 4½ rounds to 2in (5cm) measured over double crochet using a US size 7 (4.5mm) crochet hook.

ABBREVIATIONS

See page 9.

colorway c

colorway b

BAG PANELS (MAKE 2)

The Front and Back panels of all the bags are made using the same stitch pattern, but following different stripe sequences given here:

Colorway A stripe sequence

FRONT AND BACK

Foundation ring and Rounds 1, 4, and 7: Col A.
Rounds 2, 5, and 8: Col B.
Rounds 3 and 6: Col C.
Bag Strap: Col B.

Colorway B stripe sequences

FRONT

Foundation ring and Rounds 1 and 2: Col A.
Rounds 3 and 4: Col B.
Rounds 5 and 6: Col C.
Rounds 7 and 8: Col D.

BACK

Foundation ring and Rounds 1 and 2: Col D.
Rounds 3 and 4: Col C.
Rounds 5 and 6: Col B.
Rounds 7 and 8: Col A.
Bag Strap: Col D.

Colorway C stripe sequences

FRONT

Foundation ring and Rounds 1, 2, 5, and 6: Col A.
Rounds 3, 4, 7, and 8: Col B.

BACK

Foundation ring and Rounds 1, 2, 5, and 6: Col B.
Rounds 3, 4, 7, and 8: Col A.
Bag Strap: Col A.

FRONT AND BACK PANELS STITCH PATTERN

Changing colors where indicated above, work as follows:
Foundation ring: Using a US size 7 (4.5mm) crochet hook, ch 4 and join with a sl st in first ch to form a ring. Cont working in rounds, with RS always facing.
Round 1 (RS): Ch 3 (counts as first dc), 11 dc in center of ring, join with a sl st in top of 3-ch. *12 sts.*

Round 2: Ch 3 (counts as first dc), 1 dc in same place as last sl st was worked to make first inc, 2 dc in each dc to end of round, join with a sl st in top of 3-ch. *24 sts.*
Round 3: Ch 3 (counts as first dc), 2 dc in next dc, *1 dc in next dc, 2 dc in next dc; rep from * to end of round, join with a sl st in top of 3-ch. *36 sts.*
Round 4: Ch 3 (counts as first dc), 1 dc in next dc, 2 dc in next dc, *1 dc in each of next 2 dc, 2 dc in next dc; rep from * to end of round, join with a sl st in top of 3-ch. *48 sts.*
Round 5: Ch 3 (counts as first dc), 1 dc in each of next 2 dc, 2 dc in next dc, *1 dc in each of next 3 dc, 2 dc in next dc; rep from * to end of round, join with a sl st in top of 3-ch. *60 sts.*
Rounds 6–8: Cont in patt as set, inc number of single dc sts between each inc by 1 st in each round, so at end of each round the number of sts is increased by 12. *96 sts.*
Fasten off, leaving yarn tail at least 4in (10cm) long.

STRAP

Using a US size 7 (4.5mm) crochet hook, ch 50.
Cont working in rows, turning at end of each row.
Row 1: 1 sc in second ch from hook, 1 sc in each ch to end of row. *49 sc.*
Row 2: Ch 1 (does NOT count as a st), 1 sc in each sc to end of row.
Row 3: Work as Row 2.
Fasten off.

TO FINISH

Weave any loose yarn ends into the back of your work so they are not visible from the right side.
Lightly steam all pieces.
Using matching sewing thread, position the zipper between the Front and Back panels and sew securely in place.
Using cotton yarn, with wrong sides together, sew Front and Back panels together all around the outside edge of the bag, catching in the two ends of the handle at one end of the zipper. If desired, line the bag with fabric, using the crochet bag as the template for the two fabric pieces.

+ CROPPED TEE

///

YOU WILL NEED

YARN

For short version

3(3:3:3:4:4) x 113g (4oz) hanks of Jill Draper Makes Stuff *Hudson*, or a similar worsted-weight wool yarn, in bright yellow (Daffodil)

For long version

3(3:4:4:4:5) x 113g (4oz) hanks of Jill Draper Makes Stuff *Hudson*, or a similar worsted-weight wool yarn, in bright yellow (Daffodil)

CROCHET HOOK

US size H/8 (5mm) crochet hook

OTHER EQUIPMENT

Blunt-tipped yarn or tapestry needle, for weaving in yarn ends and sewing seams

GAUGE

15 sts and 10 rows to 4in (10cm) measured over double crochet using a US size H/8 (5mm) crochet hook.

ABBREVIATIONS

See page 9.

SPECIAL ABBREVIATION

sc2tog = [insert hook in next st, yo and draw a loop through] twice (3 loops now on hook), yo and draw through all 3 loops on hook to decrease one stitch.

SIZES

To fit bust (inches)	30	32	34	36	38	40
To fit bust (cm)	76	81	86	91	97	102

FINISHED MEASUREMENTS

Around bust (inches)	31½	33½	35½	37½	39¾	41¾
Around bust (cm)	80	85	90	95	101	106
Length (inches)–short version	15¼	15¼	15¾	16	16½	17
Length (cm)–short version	39	39	40	41	42	43
Length (inches)–long version	18½	18½	19	19¼	19¾	20
Length (cm)–long version	47	47	48	49	50	51
Sleeve seam (inches)	¾	¾	¾	¾	¾	¾
Sleeve seam (cm)	2	2	2	2	2	2

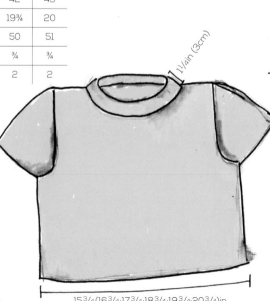

1¼in (3cm)

long version: 18½(18½:19:19¼:19¾:20)in / 47(47:48:49:50:51)cm
short version: 15¼(15¼:15¾:16:16½:17)in / 39(39:40:41:42:43)cm

15¾(16¾:17¾:18¾:19¾:20¾)in
40(42.5:45:47.5:50.5:53)cm

FRONT

Foundation chain: Using a US size H/8 (5mm) crochet hook, ch 61(65:69:73:77:81).

Cont working in rows, turning at end of each row.

Row 1 (RS): 1 dc in third ch from hook, 1 dc in each ch to end of row.

Row 2: Ch 3 (counts as first dc), skip first dc, 1 dc in each dc to end of row, ending with 1 dc in top of tch. *60(64:68:72:76:80) sts.*

Rows 3–4: Work as Row 2.

Cont in this dc patt as set until work measures 8¼(8¼:8½:9:9½:9¾)in/21(21:22:23:24:25)cm for the short version OR 11½(11½:11¾:12¼:12½:13)in/ 29(29:30:31:32:33)cm for the long version, ending with a WS row.

SHAPE ARMHOLE

Row 1 (RS): Ch 1, 1 sl st in each of first 3(4:4:5:5:5) dc, ch 3 (counts as first dc), skip 1 dc, 1 dc in each dc to last 5(6:6:7:7:7) sts, skip 1 dc, 1 dc in next dc, turn. *52(54:58:60:64:68) sts.*

Row 2: Ch 3 (counts as first dc), skip first 2 dc, 1 dc in each dc to last dc, skip last dc, 1 dc in top of tch, turn. *50(52:56:58:62:66) sts.*

Row 3: Work as Row 2. *48(50:54:56:60:64) sts.********

Cont working without shaping until work measures 12½(12½:13:13¼:13¾:14¼)in/32(32:33:34:35:36)cm for the short version OR 15¾(15¾:16¼:16½:17:17¼)in/ 40(40:41:42:43:44)cm for the long version, ending with a WS row.

SHAPE NECK

Row 1 (RS): Ch 3 (counts as first dc), skip first dc, 1 dc in each of next 13(14:15:16:17:18) dc, skip 1 dc, sc2tog over next 2 dc, 1 sl st in each of next 14(14:16:16:18:20) dc, sc2tog over next 2 dc, skip 1 dc, 1 dc in each of last 13(14:15:16:17:18) dc, 1 dc in top of tch.

Work in short rows as follows:

Row 2: Ch 3 (counts as first dc), skip first dc, 1 dc in each of next 12(13:14:15:16:17) dc, skip 1 dc, 1 dc in next st (in top of sc2tog), turn. *14(15:16:17:18:19) sts.*

Row 3: Ch 3 (counts as first dc), skip first 2 dc, 1 dc in each dc to end of row, 1 dc in top of tch, turn. *13(14:15:16:17:18) sts.*

Row 4: Ch 3 (counts as first dc), skip first dc, 1 dc in each of next 10(11:12:13:14:15) dc, skip last dc, 1 dc in top of tch, turn. *12(13:14:15:16:17) sts.*

Row 5: Ch 3 (counts as first dc), skip first 2 dc, 1 dc in each dc to end of row, 1 dc in top of tch. *11(12:13:14:15:16) sts.*

Row 6: Ch 3 (counts as first dc), skip first dc, 1 dc in each dc to end of row, 1 dc in top of tch.

Row 7: Work as Row 6.

Fasten off.

With WS facing, rejoin yarn to other side of neck, 15(16:17:18:19:20) sts from shoulder edge in top of sc2tog (remembering to count tch as a st).

Row 1 (WS): Ch 3 (counts as first dc), skip 1 dc, 1 dc in each dc to end of row, 1 dc in top of tch. *14(15:16:17:18:19) sts.*

Row 2: Ch 3 (counts as first dc), skip first dc, 1 dc in each of next 11(12:13:14:15:16) dc, skip last dc, 1 dc in top of tch, turn. *13(14:15:16:17:18) sts.*

Row 3: Ch 3 (counts as first dc), skip first 2 dc, 1 dc in each dc to end of row, 1 dc in top of tch. *12(13:14:15:16:17) sts.*

Row 4: Ch 3 (counts as first dc), skip first dc, 1 dc in each dc to last dc before neck edge, skip last dc, 1 dc in top of tch, turn. *11(12:13:14:15:16) sts.*

Row 5: Ch 3 (counts as first dc), skip first dc, 1 dc in each dc to end of row, 1 dc in top of tch.

Row 6: Work as Row 5.

Fasten off.

BACK

Work as given for Front until * * *.

Cont working without shaping until work measures 15¼(15¼:15¾:16:16½:17)in/39(39:40:41:42:43)cm for the short version OR 18½(18½:19:19¼:19¾:20)in/ 47(47:48:49:50:51)cm for the long version, ending with a WS row.

Next row (RS): Ch 3 (counts as first dc), skip first dc, 1 dc in each of next 10(11:12:13:14:15) dc.

Fasten off.

With RS facing, rejoin yarn to other side of neck, 11(12:13:14:15:16) sts from end of row (remembering to count tch as a st), ch 3 (counts as first dc), 1 dc in each dc to end of row, 1 dc in top of tch.

Fasten off.

SLEEVES (MAKE 2)

Foundation chain: Using a US size H/8 (5mm) crochet hook, ch 46(47:48:50:52:53).

Cont working in rows, turning at end of each row.

Row 1 (RS): 1 dc in fourth ch from hook, 1 dc in each ch to end of row.

Row 2: Ch 3 (counts as first dc), skip first dc, 1 dc in each dc to end of row, 1 dc in top of tch. *44(45:46:48:50:51) sts.*

SHAPE SLEEVE CAP

Row 3: Ch 1, 1 sl st in each of first 7(7:7:8:9:10) sts, ch 3 (counts as first dc), skip 1 dc , 1 dc in each dc to last 9(9:9:10:11:12) sts (remembering to count tch as a st), skip 1 dc, 1 dc in each of next 2 dc, turn. *30(31:30:32:32:31) sts.*

Row 4: Ch 3 (counts as first dc), skip first 2 dc, 1 dc in each dc to last 2 dc, skip 1 dc, 1 dc in last dc, 1 dc in top of tch. *28(29:28:30:30:29) sts.*

[Rep Row 4] 9 times more. *10(11:10:12:12:11) sts.*

Fasten off.

TO FINISH

Weave any loose yarn ends into the back of your work so they are not visible from the right side.

Lightly steam all the garment pieces.

Sew together the Back and Fronts at the shoulders.

Pin the sleeve caps into the armhole openings, then sew them in place.

Sew the Back and Fronts together along the side seams, stitching from the bottom edge of the garment up to the underarm, then down along the underarm Sleeve seams to the cuffs.

ADD NECK EDGING

With RS facing, rejoin yarn at center back of garment and work as follows:

Next round: Ch 3 (counts as first dc), work dc evenly all around neck edge, join round with a sl st in top of 3-ch.

Next round: Ch 3 (counts as first dc), 1 dc in each dc to end, join round with a sl st in top of 3-ch.

Rep last round once more.

Fasten off.

denim plaid scarf

POMPOM BERET

//

YOU WILL NEED

YARN
2 x 100g (3½oz) hanks of Misti Alpaca *Chunky*,
or a similar bulky-weight wool yarn, in lilac
(1742 California Lilac)

CROCHET HOOK
US size K/10½ (7mm) crochet hook

OTHER EQUIPMENT
Blunt-tipped yarn or tapestry needle, for weaving in yarn
ends and sewing seams

GAUGE
15 sts and 15 rounds to 4in (10cm) measured over single
crochet using a US size K/10½ (7mm) crochet hook.

ABBREVIATIONS
See page 9.

SPECIAL ABBREVIATION
sc2tog = [insert hook in next st, yo and draw a loop
through] twice (3 loops now on hook), yo and draw
through all 3 loops on hook to decrease one stitch (see
page 20).

//

BERET

Foundation ring: Using a US size K/10½ (7mm) crochet
hook, ch 4 and join with a sl st in first ch to form a ring.
Cont working in rounds, with RS always facing.
Round 1 (RS): Ch 1 (counts as first sc), 5 sc in center of
ring, join with a sl st in top of 1-ch. *6 sts.*
Round 2: Ch 1 (counts as first sc), 1 sc in same place last
sl st was worked to make first inc, 2 sc in each st to end of
round, join with a sl st in top of 1-ch. *12 sts.*
Round 3: Ch 1 (counts as first sc), 2 sc in next st, *1 sc
in next st, 2 sc in next st; rep from * to end of round, join
with a sl st in top of 1-ch. *18 sts.*
Round 4: Ch 1 (counts as first sc), 1 sc in next st, 2 sc
in next st, *1 sc in each of next 2 sts, 2 sc in next st; rep
from * to end of round, join with a sl st in top of 1-ch.
24 sts.
Round 5: Ch 1 (counts as first sc), 1 sc in each of next
2 sts, 2 sc in next st, *1 sc in each of next 3 sts, 2 sc in
next st; rep from * to end of round, join with a sl st in top
of 1-ch. *30 sts.*
Cont working in patt as set, inc the number of single sc sts
between each inc by 1 st in each round (so that at end of
each round the number of sts is increased by 6), until you
have 108 sts in a round.
Next round: Ch 1 (counts as first sc), 1 sc in each st of
round, join with a sl st in top of 1-ch.
Rep last round 7 times more.

Round 1: Ch 1 (counts as first sc), 1 sc in each of next
15 sts, sc2tog over next 2 sts, *1 sc in each of next 16 sts,
sc2tog over next 2 sts; rep from * to end of round, join
with a sl st in top of 1-ch. *102 sts.*
Round 2: Ch 1 (counts as first sc), 1 sc in each of next
14 sts, sc2tog, *1 sc in each of next 15 sts, sc2tog; rep
from * to end of round, join with a sl st in top of 1-ch.
96 sts.
Round 3: Ch 1 (counts as first sc), 1 sc in each of next 13
sts, sc2tog, *1 sc in each of next 14 sts, sc2tog; rep from *
to end of round, join with a sl st in top of 1-ch. *90 sts.*
Cont working in patt as set, dec the number of single sc
sts between each dec by 1 st in each round (so that at end
of each round the number of sts is decreased by 6), until
54 sts rem in a round.
Final round: Ch 1, 1 sc in each st of round, join with a sl
st in top of 1-ch.
Fasten off.

TO FINISH

Weave any loose yarn ends into the back of your work so
they are not visible from the right side.
Use remaining yarn to make a large pompom for the top
of the beret. If you only have a small amount of the main
color yarn left over, use a contrasting color yarn or a mix
of the main color with a contrasting color yarn.

pompom beret

+ ZIGZAG SHOPPER

SIZE: **12½ x 11¾ x 4¾in**
(32 x 30 x 12cm)

///

YOU WILL NEED

YARN
4 x 100g (3½oz) balls of Prick Your Finger *Carpet Yarn*, or a similar Aran-weight yarn, in natural

OTHER MATERIAL
Lining fabric and matching sewing thread

CROCHET HOOK
US size H/8 (5mm) crochet hook

OTHER EQUIPMENT
Blunt-tipped yarn or tapestry needle, for weaving in yarn ends and sewing seams
Sewing needle, for stitching the lining into bag

GAUGE
Achieving an exact gauge is not essential when crocheting this bag, as the finished size of the shopper can vary.

ABBREVIATIONS
See page 9.

SPECIAL ABBREVIATIONS
single dtr group = *[yo] 3 times and insert hook in sc, yo and draw a loop through, [yo and draw though first 2 loops on hook] 3 times** to make first incomplete dtr; rep from * to **twice more working each st into same sc (so you have now made a total of 3 incomplete dtr and there are 4 loops on hook), yo and draw through all 4 loops on hook.

double dtr group = *[yo] 3 times and insert hook in same sc as last group, yo and draw a loop through, [yo and draw through first 2 loops on hook] 3 times** to make first incomplete dtr; rep from * to ** twice more working each st into same sc*** (so you have now made a total of 3 incomplete dtr and there are 4 loops on hook), skip 5 sc, work 3 incomplete dtr all into next sc (7 loops now on hook), yo and draw through all 7 loops on hook.

single end dtr group = work as for *double dtr group* to *** (so you have now made a total of 3 incomplete dtr and there are 4 loops on hook), skip 2 sc, rep from * to ** of *double dtr group* once but working into last sc of row (5 loops now on hook), yo and draw through all 5 loops on hook.

DESIGN NOTE
This bag is made up of four separate panels of different yet simple crochet stitches, which are sewn together with a fabric lining.

ZIGZAG STITCH PATTERN IN SYMBOLS
See page 9 for main symbols.

Special symbols

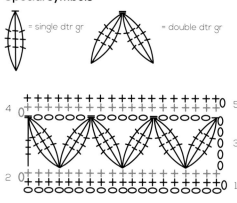

= single dtr gr   = double dtr gr

BAG BASE

Foundation chain: Using a US size H/8 (5mm) crochet hook, ch 44.

Cont working in rows, turning at end of each row.

Row 1 (RS): 1 dc in third ch from hook, 1 dc in each ch to end of row. *42 dc.*

Row 2: Ch 3 (does NOT count as first dc), 1 dc in each dc to end of row (do not work last dc of row in top of tch). *42 dc.*

Rep Row 2 until work measures approximately 5½in (14cm).

Fasten off.

MAIN PANELS (MAKE 2)

These double crochet panels form the Front and Back of the bag.

Foundation chain: Using a US size H/8 (5mm) crochet hook, ch 35.

Cont working in rows, turning at end of each row.

Row 1 (RS): 1 dc in third ch from hook, 1 dc in each ch to end of row. *33 dc.*

Row 2: Ch 3 (does NOT count as first dc), 1 dc in each dc to end of row (do not work last dc of row in top of tch). *33 dc.*

Rep Row 2 until work measures approximately 12½in (32cm).

Fasten off.

SIDE PANELS (MAKE 2)

These zigzag stitch panels form the narrow side end panels of the bag.

Foundation chain: Using a US size H/8 (5mm) crochet hook, ch 32.

Cont working in rows, turning at end of each row.

Row 1 (RS): 1 sc in second ch from hook, 1 sc in each ch to end of row. *31 sc.*

Row 2: Ch 1 (does NOT count as a st), 1 sc in each sc to end of row.

Row 3: 5 ch (counts as first dtr), skip first 3 sc, work 1 single dtr group in next sc, 5 ch, *1 double dtr group, 5 ch; rep from * to last 3 sc, work 1 single end dtr group.

Row 4: Ch 1, 1 sc in top of first group, 5 sc in 5-ch space, *1 sc in top of next group, 5 sc in next 5-ch space; rep from * to last group, 1 sc in top of 5-ch at end of row. *31 sc.*

Row 5: Ch 1, 1 sc in each sc to end of row.

Rows 2–5 form the zigzag stitch pattern.

Cont in this zigzag stitch pattern until work measures approximately 12½in (32cm), ending with a Row 2.

Fasten off.

STRAPS (MAKE 2)

Foundation chain: Using a US size H/8 (5mm) crochet hook, ch 8.

Cont working in rows, turning at end of each row.

Row 1: 1 dc in third ch from hook (2-ch at beg count as first dc), 1 dc in each ch to end of row. *6 sts.*

Row 2: Ch 3 (counts as first dc), skip first dc, 1 dc in each of remaining dc, ending with 1 dc in top of tch.

Rep Row 2 until Strap measures approximately 19½in (50cm) or preferred length. (Bear in mind that the bag straps will stretch through usage, so it is a good idea to make them slightly shorter.)

Fasten off.

TO FINISH

Weave any loose yarn ends into the back of your work so they are not visible from the right side.

Lightly steam all the pieces to ensure they lie flat.

To cut the lining pieces, draw onto the fabric around each piece (excluding the straps), adding a ½in (1.5cm) seam allowance all around, and cut out.

Sew a crocheted side panel to each side edge of a crocheted main panel, then sew the remaining main panel to the side panels to form a tube. Sew the tube to the crocheted bag base. Sew one strap to the top of each of the main panels as shown.

Stitch all the lining pieces together as for the crocheted pieces. Insert the lining into the bag, then turn under the top edge and stitch it in place around the top of the bag.

STRIPED SWEATER AND CLUTCH BAG

///

YOU WILL NEED

YARN FOR SWEATER AND CLUTCH BAG
4 x 100g (3½oz) hanks of Quince & Co. *Osprey*, or a
similar Aran-weight wool yarn, in one color:
A dark blue (Pea Coat)
1 x 100g (3½oz) hanks of Quince & Co. *Osprey*, or a
similar Aran-weight wool yarn, in each of five colors:
B dark pink (Rosa Rugosa)
C mustard (Honey)
D dark red (Malbec)
E pale beige (Chanterelle)
F light blue (Lupine)

OTHER MATERIALS FOR CLUTCH BAG
Zipper to fit top of bag
Lining fabric and matching thread

CROCHET HOOK
US size K/10½ (6.5mm) crochet hook

OTHER EQUIPMENT
Blunt-tipped yarn or tapestry needle, for weaving in yarn
ends and sewing seams
Sewing needle, for stitching the lining and zipper into
the bag

GAUGE
Four 3-dc groups and 8½ rows to 4in (10cm) measured
over granny stripe stitch pattern using a US size K/10½
(6.5mm) crochet hook.

ABBREVIATIONS
See page 9.

SIZES

To fit bust (inches)	32	34	36	38	40
To fit bust (cm)	81	86	91	97	102

FINISHED MEASUREMENTS

Around bust (inches)	40	42	44	46	48
Around bust (cm)	100	105	110	115	120
Length (inches)	19½	19½	20	20½	20¾
Length (cm)	50	50	51	52	53
Sleeve seam (inches)	18	18	18	19	19
Sleeve seam (cm)	45	45	45	47	47

18 (18:18:19:19)in
45(45:45:47:47)cm

19½(19½:20:20½:20¾)in
50(50:51:52:53)cm

20(21:22:23:24)in
50(52.5:55:57.5:60)cm

striped sweater

SWEATER

<hr>

BACK

Foundation chain: Using a US size K/10½ (6.5mm) crochet hook and Col A, ch 64(67:70:73:76). Cont working in rows, turning at end of each row.

Row 1 (RS): 1 dc in fourth ch from hook, skip 2 ch, *3 dc in next ch, skip 2 ch; rep from * to last ch, 2 dc in last ch.

****Row 2:** Ch 3, skip first 2 dc, 3 dc in first space (between second dc and first 3-dc group), *skip 3 dc, 3 dc in next space (between next two 3-dc groups); rep from * to end of row, working last 3 dc in space between last 3-dc group and last dc, 1 dc in top of 3-ch at end of row. Change to Col B.

Row 3: Ch 3, 1 dc in first space (between first dc and first 3-dc group), *skip 3 dc, 3 dc in next space (between next two 3-dc groups); rep from * to end of row, ending with skip last 3 dc, 2 dc in top of 3-ch at end of row. Change to Col C.

Row 4: Work as Row 2.
Change to Col D.

Row 5: Work as Row 3.
Change to Col E.

Row 6: Work as Row 2.
Change to Col F.

Row 7: Work as Row 3.
Change to Col A.**

Repeat from ** to ** (Rows 2–7) to form the granny stripe stitch pattern.

Cont working in this granny stripe stitch pattern until work measures 19½(19½:20:20½:20¾)in/ 50(50:51:52:53)cm.
Fasten off.

FRONT

Foundation chain: Using a US size K/10½ (6.5mm) crochet hook and Col A, ch 64(67:70:73:76). Cont working in rows, turning at end of each row. Work as for Back until work measures 16½(16½:17:17½:17¾)in/42(42:43:44:45)cm, ending with a RS row (a Row 3).

SHAPE NECK
Work each side of neck separately.

Bust sizes 32in (81cm), 36in (91cm), and 40in (102cm) only

With WS facing and changing colors as set in granny stripe stitch pattern, work right-hand side of neck as follows:

Row 1 (WS): Ch 3, 3 dc in first space and foll 7(–:8:–:9) spaces, skip 2 dc, 1 dc in next dc, turn.

Row 2: Ch 3, 3 dc in first space and foll 6(–:7:–:8) spaces, 2 dc in top of 3-ch.

Row 3: Ch 3, 3 dc in first space and foll 6(–:7:–:8) spaces, 1 dc in top of 3-ch.

Rows 4–7: Work 4 rows in granny stripe stitch pattern without shaping.
Fasten off.

With WS facing, leave a gap of 9 dc (three 3-dc groups) at center and rejoin yarn to left-hand side of neck in space before next 3-dc group, then cont working as follows:

Row 1 (WS): Ch 3, 3 dc in next space and foll 7(–:8:–:9) spaces, 1 dc in top of 3-ch.

Row 2: Ch 3, 1 dc in first space, 3 dc in next 7(–:8:–:9) spaces, 1 dc in top of 3-ch.

Row 3: Ch 3, skip first space, 3 dc in next 7(–:8:–:9) spaces, 1 dc in top of 3-ch.

Rows 4–7: Cont working straight in granny stripe stitch pattern without shaping.
Fasten off.

Bust sizes 34in (86cm) and 38in (97cm) only

With WS facing and changing colors as set in granny stripe stitch pattern, work right-hand side of neck as follows:

Row 1 (WS): Ch 3, 3 dc in first space and foll –(7:–:8:–) spaces, 2 dc in next space, turn.

Row 2: Ch 3, 1 dc in first space, 3 dc in next –(7:–:8:–) spaces, 2 dc in top of 3-ch, turn.

Row 3: Ch 3, 3 dc in next space and foll –(6:–:7:–) spaces, 1 dc in next space, 1 dc in top of 3-ch.

Rows 4–7: Work 4 rows in granny stripe stitch pattern without shaping.
Fasten off.

With WS facing, leave a gap of 12 dc (four 3-dc groups) at center and rejoin yarn to left-hand side of neck in space before nexst 3-dc group, then cont working as follows:

Row 1 (WS): Ch 3, 1 dc in same space and 3 dc in foll –(8:–:9:–) spaces, 1 dc in top of 3-ch.

Row 2: Ch 3, 1 dc in first space, 3 dc in foll –(7–:8:–) spaces, 1 dc in next space, 1 dc in top of 3-ch.

Row 3: Ch 3, 1 dc in first space, 3 dc in foll –(7:–8:–) spaces, 1 dc in top of 3-ch.

Rows 4–7: Work 4 rows in granny stripe stitch pattern without shaping.

Fasten off.

SLEEVES (MAKE 2)

Foundation chain: Using a US size K/10½ (6.5mm) crochet hook and Col A, ch 31(31:31:37:37).

Cont working in rows, turning at end of each row.

Row 1 (RS): 1 dc in fourth ch from hook, skip 2 ch, *3 dc in next ch, skip 2 ch; rep from * to last ch, 2 dc in last ch.

Row 2: Ch 3, skip first 2 dc, 3 dc in first space (between second dc and first 3-dc group), *skip 3 dc, 3 dc in next space (between next two 3-dc groups); rep from * to end of row, working last 3 dc in space between last 3-dc group and last dc, 1 dc in top of 3-ch at end of row.

Row 3: Ch 3, 1 dc in first space (between first dc and first 3-dc group), *skip 3 dc, 3 dc in next space (between next two 3-dc groups); rep from * to end of row, ending with skip last 3 dc, 2 dc in top of 3-ch at end of row.

Rows 2–3 form the stitch pattern.

Cont working in stitch pattern as set for 38(38:38:40:40) rows in total, but working inc rows on the 5th, 12th, 17th, 24th, and 29th rows as follows:

Inc row: Ch 3, 3 dc in first space (between first dc and first 3-dc group), 3 dc in all spaces to end of row, working last 3 dc in space beteen last 3-dc group and tch, 1 dc in top of 3-ch.

Note: The inc rows alter the stitch pattern at the beg and ends of each row, so after an inc row your next row will be a Row 3.

Fasten off.

TO FINISH

Weave any loose yarn ends into the back of your work so they are not visible from the right side.

Lightly steam all the garment pieces.

Sew together the Back and Front at the shoulders.

Pin the center of the top of the sleeves to the shoulder seams and stitch in place.

Sew the Back and Fronts together along the side seams, stitching from the bottom edge of the garment up to the underarm, then down along the underarm Sleeve seams to the cuffs.

ADD NECKBAND

With a US size K/10½ (6.5mm) crochet hook, join Col A to neck edge at the center back and work in rounds with RS always facing as follows:

Round 1 (RS): Ch 3, 2 dc in same space as 3-ch and work in groups of 3 dc all around neckline, join with a sl st to top of first 3-ch.

Round 2: Work as Round 1 but beg with ch 3 and work 3 dc in spaces between 3-dc groups of previous round, join with a sl st to top of first 3-ch.

Fasten off.

Weave in any loose yarn ends.

CLUTCH BAG

CLUTCH BAG PANELS (MAKE 2)

Foundation chain: Using a US size K/10½ (6.5mm) crochet hook and Col A, ch 31.

Cont working in rows, turning at end of each row.

Row 1 (RS): 1 dc in fourth ch from hook, skip 2 ch, *3 dc in next ch, skip 2 ch; rep from * to last ch, 2 dc in last ch.

****Row 2:** Ch 3, skip first 2 dc, 3 dc in first space (between second dc and next 3-dc group), *skip 3 dc, 3 dc in next space (between next two 3-dc groups); rep from * to end of row, working last 3 dc in space between last 3-dc group and last dc, 1 dc in top of 3-ch at end of row. Change to Col B.

Row 3: Ch 3, 1 dc in first space (between first dc and first 3-dc group), *skip 3 dc, 3 dc in next space (between next two 3-dc groups); rep from * to end of row, ending with skip last 3 dc, 2 dc in top of 3-ch at end of row. Change to Col C.

Row 4: Work as Row 2. Change to Col D.

Row 5: Work as Row 3. Change to Col E.

Row 6: Work as Row 2. Change to Col F.

Row 7: Work as Row 3. Change to Col A.**

Repeat from ** to ** (Rows 2–7) to form the granny stripe stitch pattern.

Cont working in this granny stripe stitch pattern until work measures approximately 7¼in (18.5cm).

Fasten off.

HANDLE

Foundation chain: Using a US size K/10½ (6.5mm) crochet hook and Col A, ch 43.

Row 1: 1 dc in fourth ch from hook, 1 dc in each ch to end of row.

Fasten off.

TO FINISH

Weave any loose yarn ends into the back of your work so they are not visible from the right side.

Lightly steam the panel pieces.

Cut two fabric lining pieces, the same size as the bag panel plus ½in (1.5cm) extra all around for the seam allowance.

Sew together the crocheted bag panel pieces, leaving the top edge open and catching in both ends of the handle together at one end.

Stitch the lining pieces together, sewing the zipper into the top seam. Insert the lining into the bag and sew it to the bag so all the raw edges are hidden and the zipper sits neatly at the opening of the bag.

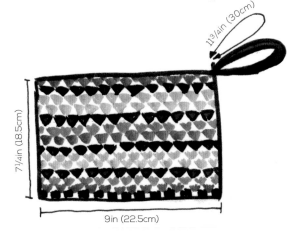

7¼in (18.5cm)

9in (22.5cm)

11¾in (30cm)

poodle slippers

POODLE SLIPPERS

YOU WILL NEED

YARN
2 x 50g (1¾oz) balls of Rowan *Pure Wool 4ply*, or a similar super-fine-weight wool yarn, in pale pink (468 Shell)
2 x 25g (⅞oz) balls of Rowan *Mohair Haze*, or a similar super-fine-weight mohair yarn, in pale pink (521 Baby)

OTHER MATERIALS
Small amount of black embroidery thread or yarn, for adding the facial features
12in (30cm) square of pink suede or a similar nonslip fabric, for soles of slippers

CROCHET HOOKS
US sizes G/6 and 7 (4mm and 4.5mm) crochet hooks

OTHER EQUIPMENT
Blunt-tipped yarn or tapestry needle, for weaving in yarn ends and sewing seams

GAUGE
18 sts and 20 rows to 4in (10cm) measured over single crochet loop stitch using a US size G/6 (4mm) hook.

ABBREVIATIONS
See page 9.

SPECIAL ABBREVIATION
single crochet loop stitch = see below for instructions.

DESIGN NOTE
One strand each of the two yarns required for these slippers are worked together at the same time throughout.

SINGLE CROCHET LOOP STITCH

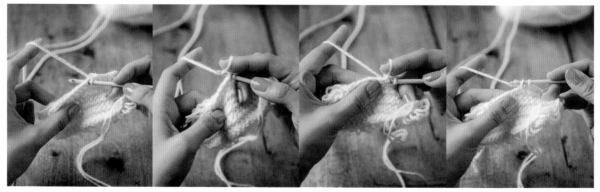

STEP 1 Loop stitch is easy to work and creates a really fun effect. It's worked on a WS row, so the loops will be seen from the right side. Insert the hook as usual into the next stitch as if starting to work a single crochet.

STEP 2 When wrapping your yarn around the hook, wrap it around your index finger at the same time to create a loop.

STEP 3 Keeping the yarn wrapped around your finger, draw the yarn through in the usual way.

STEP 4 Finish the stitch by working a yo and drawing through the remaining two loops on the hook. Remove your finger from the loop and move on to the next stitch. Once you've finished your work, tighten up your stitches by gently pulling the loops from the right side.

SNOUTS (MAKE 2)

Foundation chain: Using a US size G/6 (4mm) crochet hook and two strands of yarn, ch 9.
Cont working in rows, turning at end of each row.
Row 1 (RS): 1 sc in second ch from hook, 1 sc in each ch to end of row. *8 sc.*
Row 2: Ch 1 (does NOT count as a st), 1 single crochet loop stitch in each sc to end of row.
Row 3: Ch 1 (does NOT count as a st), 2 sc in first st, 1 sc in each st to last st of row, 2 sc in last st. *10 sc.*
Row 4: Work as Row 2.
Rows 5–20: [Rep Rows 3–4] 8 times more. *26 sts.*
Rows 21–28: [Rep Rows 3–4] 4 times more, but when working central 8 sts in single crochet loop stitch wrap yarn twice around index finger instead of once to make loops longer for shaggy hair. *34 sts.*
Row 29: Ch 1, 1 sc in each st to end of row.
Fasten off.

BACKS (MAKE 2)

Foundation chain: Using a US size G/6 (4mm) crochet hook and two strands of yarn, ch 31.
Cont working in rows, turning at end of each row.
Row 1 (RS): 1 sc in second ch from hook, 1 sc in each ch to end of row. *30 sc.*
Row 2: Ch 1 (does NOT count as a st), 1 single crochet loop stitch in each sc to end of row.
Row 3: Ch 1 (does NOT count as a st), 1 sc in each st to end of row.
Rows 4–13: [Rep Rows 2–3] 5 times more.
Row 14: Work as Row 3.
Fasten off.

EARS (MAKE 4)

Foundation chain: Using a US size 7 (4.5mm) crochet hook and two strands of yarn, ch 13.
Cont working in rows, turning at end of each row.
Row 1: 1 dc in fourth ch from hook (first 3-ch count as first dc), 1 dc in each ch to end of the row. *11 sts.*
Row 2: Ch 3 (counts as first dc), skip first dc, 1 dc in each dc to end of row, ending with 1 dc in top of 3-ch.
Rows 3–4: Rep Row 2 twice more.
Decrease across next row, using the dc2tog decrease (see page 23) as follows:
Row 5: Ch 3 (counts as first dc), skip first dc, [dc2tog over next 2 dc] 4 times, dc2tog over next 2 sts working last leg of this last dec in top of 3-ch. *6 sts.*
Fasten off.

TO FINISH

Weave any loose yarn ends into the back of your work so they are not visible from the right side.
Stitch the side edges of the Backs to the tops of the Snouts, creating the openings for your feet.
Draw roughly around your feet onto the piece of suede, creating shapes for the soles of the slippers. Cut these pieces out and pin them in place around the slipper bases, then sew in place.
Pin the Ears in place on either side of the longer loops on the Snouts and sew securely in place.
Using black embroidery thread, add two eyes and a nose to each slipper in satin stitch.

TWEED CARDIGAN

///

YOU WILL NEED

YARN
8(8:8:8:9) x 100g (3½oz) balls of Rico Design *Fashion Colour Touch*, or a similar super-bulky-weight wool yarn, in multi colors (004 Yellow Mix)

OTHER MATERIALS
Five 1in (2.5cm) buttons

CROCHET HOOK
US size M-N/13 (9mm) crochet hook

OTHER EQUIPMENT
Blunt-tipped yarn or tapestry needle, for weaving in yarn ends and sewing seams

GAUGE
9½ sts and 8 rows to 4in (10cm) measured over half double pattern using a US size M-N/13 (9mm) crochet hook.

ABBREVIATIONS
See page 9.

SPECIAL ABBREVIATION
hdc2tog = [yo, insert hook in next st, yo and draw a loop through] twice (5 loops now on hook), yo and draw through all 5 loops on hook to decrease one stitch (see page 22).

SIZES

To fit bust (inches)	32	34	36	38	40
To fit bust (cm)	81	86	91	97	102

FINISHED MEASUREMENTS

Around bust (inches)	33	35	37	39½	41½
Around bust (cm)	84	89	94	100	105
Length (inches)	19¼	19¼	19¼	19¼	19¼
Length (cm)	49	49	49	49	49
Sleeve seam (inches)	14	14	14	14	14
Sleeve seam (cm)	36	36	36	36	36

14in (36cm)

19¼in (49cm)

12⅝(13⅝:14⅝:15¾:16¾)in
32(34.5:37:40:42.5)cm

BACK

Begin by working the rib, which is crocheted horizontally across body.

Foundation chain: Using a US size M-N/13 (9mm) crochet hook, ch 9.

Cont working in rows, turning at end of each row.

Row 1 (RS): 1 sc in second ch from hook, 1 sc in each ch to end of row. *8 sc.*

Row 2: Ch 1 (does NOT count as a st), inserting hook under both loops of each sc, 1 sl st in each of next 8 sc.

Row 3: Ch 1 (does NOT count as a st), inserting hook under both loops of each sl st, 1 sc in each of next 8 sl sts.

[Rep Rows 2–3] 21(23:25:27:29) times more, but do not turn at end of last row.

With RS facing, turn rib on its side and ch 1, then work 29(31:33:36:38) sc evenly across long edge.

Row 1 (WS): Ch 2 (counts as first hdc), skip first sc, 1 hdc in each sc to end of row. *29(31:33:36:38) sts.*

Row 2: Ch 2 (counts as first hdc), skip first hdc, 1 hdc in each hdc to end of row, 1 hdc in top of t-ch.

Last row forms the hdc patt.

Row 3: Work as Row 2.

Row 4: Ch 2 (counts as first hdc), skip first hdc, 2 hdc in next hdc, 1 hdc in each hdc to last hdc, 2 hdc in last hdc, 1 hdc in top of tch. *31(33:35:38:40) sts.*

Rows 5–9: Work 5 rows as Row 2.

Row 10: Work as Row 4. *33(35:37:40:42) sts.*

Rows 11–15: Work 5 rows as Row 2.

Row 16: Work as Row 4. *35(37:39:42:44) sts.*

Rows 17–18: Work 2 rows as Row 2.

SHAPE ARMHOLE

Row 19 (WS): Ch 1, l sl st in each of first 4 hdc, ch 2 (counts as first hdc), hdc2tog, 1 hdc in each hdc to last 6 sts (remembering to count tch as a st), hdc2tog, 1 hdc in next hdc, turn. *27(29:31:34:36) sts.*

Row 20: Ch 2 (counts as first hdc), skip first hdc, 1 hdc in each hdc to end of row, 1 hdc in top of tch.

Row 21: Ch 2 (counts as first hdc), skip first hdc, hdc2tog, 1 hdc in each hdc to last 2 hdc, hdc2tog, 1 hdc in top of tch. *25(27:29:32:34) sts.*

Rows 22–23: Work as Rows 20–21. *23(25:27:30:32) sts.*

Rows 24–32: Work 9 rows as Row 20.

SHAPE SHOULDER

Work each side separately.

Row 33 (WS): Ch 2 (counts as 1 hdc), skip first hdc, 1 hdc in each of next 5(6:7:8:9) hdc, turn.

Row 34: Ch 2 (counts as 1 hdc), skip first hdc, 1 hdc in next 2(3:3:4:4) hdc.

Fasten off.

With WS facing, rejoin yarn 6(7:8:9:10) sts from side edge (remembering to count tch as a st).

Row 33 (WS): Ch 2 (counts as first hdc), 1 hdc in each hdc to end of row, 1 hdc in top of tch, turn.

Row 34: Ch 1, 1 sl st in each of first 4(4:5:5:6) hdc, ch 2 (counts as first hdc), 1 hdc in each of next 1(2:2:3:3) hdc, 1 hdc in top of tch.

Fasten off.

LEFT FRONT

Begin by working the rib, which is crocheted horizontally across body.

Foundation chain: Using a US size M-N/13 (9mm) crochet hook, ch 9.

Cont working in rows, turning at end of each row.

Row 1 (RS): 1 sc in second ch from hook, 1 sc in each ch to end of row. *8 sc.*

Row 2: Ch 1 (does NOT count as a st), inserting hook under both loops of each sc, 1 sl st in each of next 8 sc.

Row 3: Ch 1 (does NOT count as a st), inserting hook under both loops of each sl st, 1 sc in each of next 8 sl sts.

[Rep Rows 2–3] 11(12:13:14:15) times more, but do not turn at end of last row.

With RS facing, turn rib on its side and ch 1, then work 15(16:17:18:19) sc evenly across long edge.

Row 1 (WS): Ch 2 (counts as first hdc), skip first sc, 1 hdc in each sc to end of row. *15(16:17:18:19) sts.*

Rows 2: Ch 2 (counts as first hdc), skip first hdc, 1 hdc in each hdc to end of row, 1 hdc in top of tch.

Last row forms the hdc patt.

Row 3: Work as Row 2.

Row 4: Ch 2 (counts as first hdc), skip first hdc, 2 hdc in next hdc, 1 hdc in each hdc to end of row, 1 hdc in top of tch. *16(17:18:19:20) sts.*

Rows 5–9: Work 5 rows as Row 2.

Row 10: Work as Row 4. *17(18:19:20:21) sts.*

Rows 11–15: Work 5 rows as Row 2.

Row 16: Work as Row 4. *18(19:20:21:22) sts.*

Rows 17–18: Work 2 rows as Row 2.

SHAPE ARMHOLE

Row 19 (WS): Ch 2 (counts as first hdc), skip first hdc, 1 hdc in each hdc until 6 sts rem (remembering to count tch as a st), hdc2tog, 1 hdc in next hdc, turn. *14(15:16:17:18) sts.*

Row 20: Ch 2 (counts as first hdc), skip first hdc, 1 hdc in each hdc to end of row, 1 hdc in top of tch.

Row 21: Ch 2 (counts as first hdc), skip first hdc, 1 hdc in each hdc to last 2 hdc, hdc2tog, 1 hdc in top of tch. *13(14:15:16:17) sts.*

Row 22–23: Work as Rows 20–21. *12(13:14:15:16) sts.*

Rows 24–28: Work 5 rows as Row 20.

NECK SHAPING

Row 29 (WS): Ch 1, 1 sl st in each of first 3 hdc, ch 2 (counts as first hdc), hdc2tog, 1 hdc in each hdc to end of row, 1 hdc in top of tch.

Row 30: Ch 2 (counts as first hdc), skip first hdc, 1 hdc in each hdc to last 2 hdc, hdc2tog, 1 hdc in top of tch.

Row 31: Ch 2 (counts as first hdc), skip first hdc, hdc2tog, 1 hdc in each hdc to end of row, 1 hdc in top of tch.

Row 32: Work as Row 30. *6(7:8:9:10) sts.*

SHAPE SHOULDER

Row 33 (WS): Work as Row 20.

Row 34: Ch 1, 1 sl st in each of first 4(4:5:5:6) hdc, ch 2 (counts as first hdc), 1 hdc in each of next 1(2:2:3:3) hdc, 1 hdc in top of tch.

Fasten off.

RIGHT FRONT

Begin by working the rib, which is crocheted horizontally across body.

Foundation chain: Using a US size M-N/13 (9mm) crochet hook, ch 9.

Cont working in rows, turning at end of each row.

Row 1 (RS): 1 sc in second ch from hook, 1 sc in each ch to end of row. *8 sc.*

Row 2: Ch 1 (does NOT count as a st), inserting hook under both loops of each sc, 1 sl st in each of next 8 sc.

Row 3: Ch 1 (does NOT count as a st), inserting hook under both loops of each sl st, 1 sc in each of next 8 sl sts. [Rep Rows 2–3] 10(11:12:13:14) times more.

Cont to work buttonhole as follows:

Next row (WS): Ch 1, 1 sl st in each of next 3 sc, ch 2, skip 2 sc, 1 sl st in each of last 3 sc.

Next row: Ch 1 (does NOT count as a st), 1 sc in each of next 8 sts, do not turn.

With RS facing, turn rib on its side and ch 1, then work 15(16:17:18:19) sc evenly across long edge.

Row 1 (WS): Ch 2 (counts as first hdc), skip first sc, 1 hdc in each sc to end of row. *15(16:17:18:19) sts.*

Row 2: Ch 2 (counts as first hdc), skip first hdc, 1 hdc in each hdc to end of row, 1 hdc in top of tch.

Last row forms the hdc patt.

Row 3: Ch 2 (counts as first hdc), skip first hdc, 1 hdc in each hdc to last hdc, ch 1 (to form a buttonhole), skip last hdc, 1 hdc in top of tch.

Row 4: Ch 2 (counts as first hdc), skip first hdc, 1 hdc in 1-ch sp, 1 hdc each hdc to last hdc, 2 hdc in last hdc, 1 hdc in top of tch. *16(17:18:19:20) sts.*

Rows 5–8: Work 4 rows as Row 2.

Row 9: Work as Row 3.

Row 10: Work as Row 4. *17(18:19:20:21) sts.*

Rows 11–14: Work 4 rows as Row 2.

Row 15: Work as Row 3.

Row 16: Work as Row 4. *18(19:20:21:22) sts.*

Rows 17–18: Work 2 rows as Row 2.

SHAPE ARMHOLE

Row 19: (WS): Ch 1, l sl st in each of first 4 hdc, ch 2 (counts as first hdc), hdc2tog, 1 hdc in each hdc to end of row, 1 hdc in top of tch. *14(15:16:17:18) sts.*

Row 20: Ch 2 (counts as first hdc), skip first hdc, 1 hdc in each st to end of row, 1 hdc in top of tch.

Row 21: Ch 2 (counts as first hdc), skip first hdc, hdc2tog, 1 hdc in each hdc to last hdc, ch 1, skip last hdc, 1 hdc in top of tch. *13(14:15:16:17) sts.*

Row 22: Ch 2 (counts as first hdc), skip first hdc, 1 hdc in 1-ch sp, 1 hdc each hdc to end, 1 hdc in top of tch.

Row 23: Ch 2 (counts as first hdc), skip first hdc, hdc2tog, 1 hdc in each hdc to end, 1 hdc in top of tch. *12(13:14:15:16) sts.*

Rows 24–26: Work 3 rows as Row 20.

Row 27: Work as Row 3.

Row 28: Work as Row 22.

SHAPE NECK

Row 29 (WS): Ch 2 (counts as first hdc), 1 hdc in each hdc to last 5 sts (remembering to count tch as a st), hdc2tog, 1 hdc in next hdc, turn.

Row 30: Ch 2 (counts as first hdc), skip first hdc, hdc2tog, 1 hdc in each hdc to end of row, 1 hdc in top of tch.

Row 31: Ch 2 (counts as first hdc), skip first hdc, 1 hdc in each hdc to last 2 hdc, hdc2tog, 1 hdc in top of tch.

Row 32: Work as Row 30. *6(7:8:9:10) sts.*

SHAPE SHOULDER

Row 33: Work as Row 20.

Row 34: Ch 2 (counts as first hdc), skip first hdc, 1 hdc in each of next 2(3:3:4:4) hdc.

Fasten off.

SLEEVES (MAKE 2)

Begin by working the rib, which is crocheted horizontally around the wrist.

Foundation chain: Using a US size M-N/13 (9mm) crochet hook, ch 9.

Cont working in rows, turning at end of each row.

Row 1 (RS): 1 sc in second ch from hook, 1 sc in each ch to end of row. *8 sc.*

Row 2: Ch 1 (does NOT count as a st), inserting hook under both loops of each sc, 1 sl st in each of next 8 sc.

Row 3: Ch 1 (does NOT count as a st), inserting hook under both loops of each sl st, 1 sc in each of next 8 sl sts. Rep Rows 2–3] 10(11:12:13:13) times more, but do not turn at end of last row.

With RS facing, turn rib on its side and ch 1, then work 18(19:20:21:21) sc evenly across long edge.

Row 1 (WS): Ch 2 (counts as first hdc), skip first sc, 1 hdc in each sc to end of row. *18(19:20:21:21) sts.*

Row 2: Ch 2 (counts as first hdc), skip first hdc, 1 hdc in each hdc to end of row, 1 hdc in top of tch.

Last row forms the hdc patt.

Row 3: Work as Row 2.

Row 4: Ch 2 (counts as first hdc), skip first hdc, 2 hdc in next hdc, 1 hdc in each hdc to last hdc, 2 hdc in last hdc, 1 hdc in top of tch. *20(21:22:23:23) sts.*

Rows 5–22: [Rep Rows 2–4] 6 times more. *32(33:34:35:35) sts.*

Row 24: Work as Row 2.

SHAPE SLEEVE CAP

Row 25 (WS): Ch 1, 1 sl st in each of first 4 hdc, ch 2 (counts as first hdc), hdc2tog, 1 hdc in each st to last 6 sts (remembering to count tch as a st), hdc2tog, 1 hdc in next hdc, turn. *24(25:26:27:27) sts.*

Row 26: Ch 2 (counts as first hdc), skip first hdc, hdc2tog, 1 hdc in each hdc to last 2 hdc, hdc2tog, 1 hdc in top of tch. *22(23:24:25:25) sts.*

[Rep Row 26] 10 times more. *2(3:4:5:5) sts.*

Fasten off.

TO FINISH

Weave any loose yarn ends into the back of your work so they are not visible from the right side.

Lightly steam all the garment pieces.

Sew together the Back and Fronts at the shoulders.

Pin the sleeve caps into the armhole openings, then sew them in place.

Sew the Back and Fronts together along the side seams, stitching from the bottom rib edge of the garment up to the underarm, then down along the underarm Sleeve seams to the rib cuffs.

Sew buttons on the Left Front to correspond with the buttonholes on the Right Front.

LOVE TO
CROCHET

GRANNY SQUARE COTTON TEE

YOU WILL NEED

YARN

Rico Design *Essentials Cotton DK*, or a similar double-knitting-weight cotton yarn, in three colors:
A 10 x 50g (1¾oz) balls in white (80 White)
B 6 x 50g (1¾oz) balls in blue (34 Medium Blue)
C 2 x 50g (1¾oz) balls in orange (87 Pumpkin)

CROCHET HOOK

US size G/6 (4mm) crochet hook

OTHER EQUIPMENT

Blunt-tipped yarn or tapestry needle, for weaving in yarn ends and sewing seams

GAUGE

One finished and blocked Meadow Square measures 3⅛in (8cm) square using a US size G/6 (4mm) hook.

ABBREVIATIONS

See page 9.

DESIGN NOTE

This top is simple to make but once you've completed all your Meadow Squares it takes time to sew them together. You need to make a total of 90 squares—35 squares each for the Front and Back, then 10 squares for each Sleeve.

Round 2: 1 sl st in first 2-ch sp, work one petal [1 sc, 3 dc, 1 sc] in each 2-ch sp to end of round, join with a sl st in back of base of sc at beg of round. *6 petals.*
Cont working next round at back of work.
Round 3: Ch 3, skip first petal, *1 sl st in back of base of first sc of next petal, ch 3; rep from * to end of round, join with a sl st in first ch of round. *Six 3-ch sps.*
Round 4: 1 sl st in first 3-ch sp, work one petal [1 sc, 5 dc, 1 sc] in each 3-ch sp to end of round, join with a sl st in back of base of sc at beg of round. *6 petals.*
Change to Col A.
Numbering petals from start of round, work Round 5 as follows:
Round 5: Ch 3, skip first petal, 1 sl st in back of center st of second petal, ch 3, skip third petal, 1 sl st in back of first sc of fourth petal, ch 3, 1 sl st in back of center st of fifth petal, ch 3, join with a sl st in first ch of round.
Four 3-ch sps.
Round 6: Ch 3 (counts as 1 dc), [2 dc, ch 3, 3 dc] in 3-ch sp at base of 3-ch, ch 1, *[3 dc, ch 3, 3 dc] in next 3-ch sp, ch 1; rep from * twice more, join with a sl st in top of 3-ch at beg of round.

MEADOW SQUARE (MAKE 90)

Foundation ring: Using a US size G/6 (4mm) crochet hook and Col B, ch 4 and join with a sl st in first ch to form ring. Cont working in rounds, with RS always facing.
Round 1 (RS): Ch 5 (counts as 1 dc and 2-ch), *1 dc in center of ring, ch 2; rep from *4 times more, join with a sl st in third ch of 5-ch.

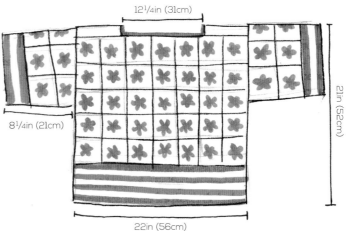

12¼in (31cm)

8¼in (21cm)

21in (52cm)

22in (56cm)

Round 7: Sl st to next 3-ch sp, ch 3 (counts as 1 dc), [2 dc, ch 3, 3 dc] in 3-ch sp at base of 3-ch, ch 1, 3 dc in next 1-ch sp, ch 1, *[3 dc, ch 3, 3 dc] in next corner 3-ch sp, ch 1, 3 dc in next 1-ch sp, ch 1; rep from * twice more, join with a sl st in top of 3-ch at beg of round.

Round 8: Sl st to next 3-ch sp, ch 3 (counts as 1 dc), [2 dc, ch 3, 3 dc] in 3-ch sp at base of 3-ch, ch 1, [3 dc in next 1-ch sp, ch 1] twice, *[3 dc, ch 3, 3 dc] in next corner 3-ch sp, ch 1, [3 dc in next 1-ch sp, ch 1] twice; rep from * twice more, join with a sl st in top of 3-ch at beg of round. Fasten off.

TO FINISH

BLOCK THE MEADOW SQUARES

Spray block each individual Meadow Square to even out the stitches and achieve a perfectly square shape. Place each square on a blocking mat or flat surface covered with a towel, then spray each square with a generous amount of water. Pin the corners of each square to the blocking mat, making sure each side measures 3⅛in (8cm) and opposite sides are parallel. Add more pins along each edge of the squares to keep them straight. Once the squares completely dry, remove the pins.

JOIN THE MEADOW SQUARES

Once you have finished and blocked all 90 squares, stitch together five rows of seven squares and then stitch these five rows together along the long edges to create a block of 35 squares for the Front. Repeat with another 35 squares for the Back. For the Sleeves, stitch together two rows of five squares and then stitch these squares together along the long edge to create a block of 10 squares. Repeat for the second Sleeve.

ADD STRIPED EDGING

With RS facing and using a US size G/6 (4mm) crochet hook, join Col C to 3-ch sp at beg of bottom edge of Front panel and work along edge of seven squares as follows:

Row 1 (RS): Ch 2, 1 sc in same 3-ch sp, 1 sc in each st and seam along edge, 1 sc in last 3-ch sp, turn. *113 sts.*

Row 2: Ch 3 (does NOT count as first dc), 1 dc in each st to end of row, turn.

Row 3: Work as Row 2.

Rows 4–5: Change to Col A, rep Rows 2–3.

Rows 6–7: Change to Col C, rep Rows 2–3.

Rep rows 4–7 twice more, finishing with a Col C stripe. Fasten off.

Repeat on Back panel.

With RS facing and using a US size G/6 (4mm) crochet hook, join Col C to 3-ch sp at beg of bottom edge of one Sleeve panel and work along edge of five squares as follows:

Row 1 (RS): Ch 2, 1 sc in same 3-ch space, 1 sc in each st and seam along edge, 1 sc in last 3-ch sp, turn. *81 sts.*

Row 2: Ch 3 (does NOT count as first dc), 1 dc in each st to end of row, turn.

Row 3: Work as Row 2.

Rows 4–5: Change to Col A, rep Rows 2–3.

Rows 6–7: Change to Col C, rep Rows 2–3.

Fasten off.

Repeat on other Sleeve panel.

SHAPE NECK ON FRONT AND BACK PANELS

With WS facing and using a US size G/6 (4mm) crochet hook, join Col A to 3-ch sp at beg of top edge of Front panel and work along edge of seven squares as follows:

Row 1 (WS): Ch 2, 1 sc in same 3-ch sp, 1 sc in each st and seam along edge, 1 sc in last 3-ch sp, turn. *113 sts.*

Next row: Ch 3 (counts as first dc), skip first sc, 1 dc in each of next 27 sc, turn. *28 sts.*

Next row: Ch 3 (counts as first dc), skip first dc, 1 dc in each dc to end of row, 1 dc in top of tch.

Fasten off.

With RS facing, rejoin Col A to 28th sc from other edge of Front, and work as follows:

Next row (RS): Ch 3 (counts as first dc), 1 dc in each of next 27 sc. *(28 sts)*

Next row: Ch 3 (counts as first dc), skip first dc, 1 dc in each dc to end of row, 1 dc in top of tch at neck edge.

Fasten off.

Repeat on Back panel.

SEW FINAL SEAMS

Weave any loose yarn ends into the back of your work so they are not visible from the right side.

Lightly steam all the garment pieces.

Sew together the Back and Fronts at the shoulders.

Pin the center of the tops of the Sleeves to the shoulder seams and stitch the tops of the Sleeves in place.

Sew the Back and Fronts together along the side seams, stitching from the bottom edge of the garment up to the underarm, then down along the underarm Sleeve seams to the cuffs.

ADD NECK EDGING

With RS facing and using a US size G/6 (4mm) crochet hook, join Col C to any st along back of neckline, ch 2, work 1 sc in each st around neckline, join round with a sl st in top of 2-ch.

Fasten off.

Weave in any loose yarn ends.

+VINTAGE-STYLE EMBROIDERED TOP

YOU WILL NEED

YARN
8(8:8:9:9) x 50g (1¾oz) balls of Drops *Alpaca 4ply*, or a similar fine-weight wool yarn, in pale blue (6205 Light Blue)

OTHER MATERIALS
Wool embroidery threads in selection of colors

CROCHET HOOK
US size D/3 (3.25mm) crochet hook

OTHER EQUIPMENT
Blunt-tipped yarn or tapestry needle, for weaving in yarn ends and sewing seams
Embroidery needle

GAUGE
3½ full 9-dc shells to 3¾in (9.5cm) and 17 rows to 4in (10cm) measured over shell stitch pattern using a US size D/3 (3.25mm) crochet hook.

ABBREVIATIONS
See page 9.

FRONT
Foundation row: Using a US size D/3 (3.25mm) crochet hook, ch 106(114:122:130:138:146).
Cont working in rows, turning at end of each row.
Row 1 (RS): 1 sc in second ch from hook, *skip 3 ch, 9 dc in next ch (called a 9-dc shell), skip 3 ch, 1 sc in next ch; rep from * to end. *13(14:15:16:17:18) 9-dc shells.*
Row 2: Ch 3 (counts as first dc), 1 dc in first sc, *ch 5, skip 9-dc shell, work a V-st of [1 dc, ch 1, 1 dc] in next sc; rep from * to last 9-dc shell, ending ch 5, skip last 9-dc shell, 2 dc in last sc.
Row 3: Ch 3 (counts as first dc), 4 dc in first dc, *working over next 5-ch to enclose it, work 1 sc in fifth dc of 9-dc shell in row below**, 9-dc shell in 1-ch sp at center of next V-st; rep from * ending last rep at **, 5 dc in top of tch.
Row 4: Ch 3, skip 5 dc, V-st in next sc, *ch 5, skip 9-dc shell, V-st in next sc; rep from * ending ch 2, 1 sl st in top of tch.

SIZES

To fit bust (inches)	30	32	34	36	38	40
To fit bust (cm)	76	81	86	91	97	102

FINISHED MEASUREMENTS

Around bust (inches)	36½	38½	40½	43	45	47
Around bust (cm)	92	98	103	108	114	120
Length (inches)	19	19	19	20	20	21
Length (cm)	48	48	48	50	50	52

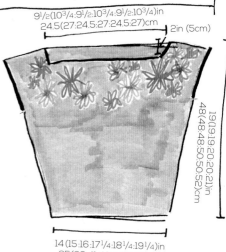

20¼(21½:22½:23½:24¾:25¾)in
51.5(54:57:60:62.5:65)cm

9½(10¾:9½:10¾:9½:10¾)in
24.5(27:24.5:27:24.5:27)cm

2in (5cm)

19(19:19:20:20:21)in
48(48:48:50:50:52)cm

14(15:16:17¼:18¼:19¼)in
35(38:41:43.5:46:49)cm

Row 5: Ch 1, 1 sc in sl st, *work 9-dc shell in 1-ch sp at center of next V-st**, working over next 5-ch to enclose it, work 1 sc in fifth dc of 9-dc shell in row below; rep from * ending last rep at **, 1 sc in third of 3-ch at end of row.

[Rep rows 2–5] 3(3:3:4:4:5) times more.

Work a set of inc rows as follows:

Row 1: Work as Row 2 of stitch pattern.

Row 2: Work as Row 3 of stitch pattern, but working 3rd(3rd:4th:4th:5th:5th) 9-dc shell by working [5 dc, ch 1, 5 dc] in sp where 9 dc would go, cont in stitch pattern until 3rd(3rd:4th:4th:5th:5th) full 9-dc shells from end and work in the same way [5 dc, ch 1, 5 dc], work to end of row.

Row 3: Work as Row 4 of stitch pattern, but when you reach split shells work [ch 5, V-st in 1-ch sp in between two 5 dc, ch 5].

Row 4: Work as Row 5 of stitch pattern, but work sc enclosing 5-ch at each side of each of incs in third dc of 5-dc group in row below.

Work Rows 2–5 of stitch pattern without shaping 4 times more.

Work inc Rows 1–4 once more.

Work Rows 2–5 of stitch pattern without shaping 4 times more.

Work inc Rows 1–4 once more.***

Work Rows 2–5 of stitch pattern without shaping 3 times more.

Next row (WS): Work as Row 2 of stitch pattern, but in place of 5-ch between V-sts work [ch 2, 1 sl st in fifth dc of 9-dc shell, ch 2].

SHAPE NECK

Work each side or neck separately.

Row 1: Work as Row 3 of stitch pattern, but work [9-dc shells] 5(5:6:6:7:7) times, then 2 dc in 1-ch sp of next V-st, turn.

Row 2: Ch 3, 1 sl st in fifth dc of first 9-dc shell, ch 2, V-st in between shells, work as Row 4 of stitch pattern to end of row.

Row 3: Work as Row 5 of stitch pattern, working [9-dc shells] 5(5:6:6:7:7) times, 1 sc in sl st of previous row. Next work Rows 2–5 of stitch pattern once more and then work final row as follows:

Next row (WS): Work as Row 2 of stitch pattern, but in place of 5-ch between V-sts work [ch 2, 1 sl st in fifth dc of 9-dc shell, ch 2].

Fasten off.

Row 1: With RS facing, rejoin yarn to other side of neck in 1-ch sp of V-st 6(6:7:7:8:8) full 9-dc shells from end of row, ch 3, 1 dc in 1-ch sp of same V-st, 1 sc in next sl st between V-sts, working as Row 3 of stitch pattern, work [9-dc shells] 5(5:6:6:7:7) times, then 5 dc in top of tch, turn.

Row 2: Working as Row 4 of stitch pattern, work to last V-st, ch 2, 1 sl st in fifth dc of 9-dc shell, 1 dc in top of tch, turn.

Row 3: Ch 2, 1 sc in sl st of previous row, work as Row 5 of stitch pattern, working [9-dc shells] 5(5:6:6:7:7) times. Next work Rows 2–5 of stitch pattern once more and then work final row as follows:

Next row (WS): Work as Row 2 of stitch pattern, but in place of 5-ch between V-sts work [ch 2, 1 sl st to fifth dc of 9-dc shell, ch 2].

Fasten off.

BACK

Foundation chain: Using a US size D/3 (3.25mm) crochet hook, ch 106(114:122:130:138:146).

Work as Front patt until ***.

Work rows 2–5 of stitch pattern without shaping 5 times more.

Next row (WS): Work as Row 2 of stitch pattern, but in place of 5-ch between V-sts work [ch 2, 1 sl st to fifth dc of 9-dc shell, ch 2].

Fasten off.

TO FINISH

Weave any loose yarn ends into the back of your work so they are not visible from the right side.

Lightly steam both garment pieces.

Sew together the Back and Front at the shoulders.

Next, sew the side seams, leaving openings for the armholes. The armhole openings can be as wide as you like; I prefer to leave the top third unstitched for the armhole openings so the top drapes nicely.

Work a round of single crochet around the neckline and the armhole openings in either the main color or a contrasting color yarn.

Add some embroidery stitches to the Front of the top in whichever designs and colors you prefer. I embroidered clusters of chain stitches in varying sizes and shades to form the floral motifs, which is really quick and easy way of adding splashes of color to your crochet.

FLORAL SUMMER TOP

YOU WILL NEED

YARN

2 x 245g (8⅝oz) cones of Yeoman Yarns *Cannele 4ply*, or a similar super-fine-weight cotton yarn, in white (6 White)

CROCHET HOOK

US size 1/0 (2.5mm) crochet hook

OTHER EQUIPMENT

Blunt-tipped yarn or tapestry needle, for weaving in yarn ends and sewing seams

GAUGE

One finished and blocked Large Floral Motif measures 2⅜in (6cm) in diameter using a size US size 1/0 (2.5mm) crochet hook.

ABBREVIATIONS

See page 9.

SPECIAL ABBREVIATIONS AND TECHNIQUES

magic circle = to make a magic circle for your foundation ring, start making a slip knot but do not tighten the starting loop (see page 10)—the stitches of the first round are worked into the open loop and then the loop is tightened.

trtr (triple treble) = yo 4 times and insert hook in chain space, yo and draw a loop through (6 loops now on hook), [yo and draw through first 2 loops on hook] 6 times to complete trtr (one loop left on hook).

DESIGN NOTE

This top is simple to make but once you have completed all your Large and Small Floral Motifs it takes time to sew them all together.

Placement of Large Floral Motifs

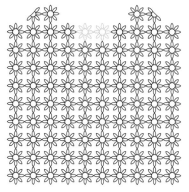

Placement of Small Floral Motifs

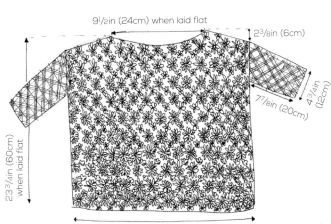

9½in (24cm) when laid flat

2⅜in (6cm)

7⅞in (20cm)

4¾in (12cm)

23¾in (60cm) when laid flat

23¾in (60cm) when laid flat

LARGE FLORAL MOTIF (MAKE 184)

Foundation ring: Using a US size 1/0 (2.5mm) hook, make a magic circle (see page 95).

Cont working in rounds, with RS always facing.

Round 1 (RS): Ch 1, 8 sc in magic circle, pull center loop tight and join with a sl st in top of first sc.

Round 2: Ch 4 (counts as first hdc and 2-ch), *1 hdc in next sc, ch 2; rep from * 6 times more, join with a sl st in second ch of 4-ch. *Eight 2-ch sps.*

Round 3: Ch 1, *[1 sc, ch 6, 1 trtr, ch 6, 1 sc] in next 2-ch sp; rep from * 7 times more, join with a sl st in top of first sc. Fasten off.

SMALL FLORAL MOTIF (MAKE 171)

Foundation ring: Using a US size 1/0 (2.5mm) hook, make a magic circle (see page 95).

Cont working in rounds, with RS always facing.

Round 1 (RS): Ch 1, [1 sc, ch 2, 1 dc, ch 2, 1 sc] 5 times in magic circle, pull center loop tight and join with a sl st in top of first sc. Fasten off.

SLEEVES (MAKE 2)

Using a US size 1/0 m (2.5m) crochet hook, ch 62.

Cont working in rows, turning at end of each row.

Row 1: 1 sc in second ch from hook, *ch 2, in same ch as 1 sc work 1 dc until 2 loops rem on hook, skip 3 ch, work 1 dc in next ch until 3 loops rem on hook, yo and draw through all 3 loops, ch 2, 1 sc in same ch as last dc (one cluster made); rep from * to end of row. *15 clusters.*

Row 2: Ch 3 (counts as first dc), work 1 dc in top of first cl, *ch 2, in same cl as last dc work [1 sc, ch 2, 1 dc until 2 loops rem on hook], 1 dc in top of next cl until 3 loops rem on hook, yo and draw through all 3 loops; rep from * to end placing last dc of last rep in last sc.

Row 3: Ch 1, in first cl work [1 sc, ch 2, 1 dc until 2 loops rem on hook], 1 dc in top of next cl until 3 loops rem on hook, yo and draw through all 3 loops, *ch 2, in same cl as last dc work [1 sc, ch 2, 1 dc until 2 loops rem on hook], 1 dc in next cl until 3 loops rem on hook, yo and draw through all 3 loops; rep from * to end placing last dc of last rep in last dc, ch 2, 1 sc in top of 3-ch at end of row. Rows 2 and 3 form stitch pattern for Sleeve.

Rows 4–5: Rep Rows 2–3 one more time.

Work incs as follows:

Row 6: Ch 4 (counts as 1 dc + 1-ch), cont in stitch pattern as set to end of row.

Row 7: Ch 2, cont in stitch pattern as set to end of row, working last sc in third ch of 4-ch at beg of previous row.

Row 8: Ch 4 (counts as 1 dc + 1-ch), work in stitch pattern as set to end of row, placing last dc in second ch of 2-ch at beg of previous row.

Row 9: Rep Row 7.

The number of clusters remains same throughout but as Sleeve widens more edge sts become longer—replace first dc with a tr and first "ch 2" with "ch 3" of each row as follows:

Row 10: Ch 3 (counts as 1 dc + 1-ch), work 1 tr in top of first cl, ch 3, cont in stitch pattern as set to end of row, placing last dc in second ch of 2-ch at beg of previous row.

Row 11: Ch 2, in first cl work [1 sc, ch 3, 1 tr until 2 loops rem on hook], cont in stitch pattern as set to end of row, working last sc in third ch of 4-ch at beg of previous row.

Rows 12–16: Rep Rows 10–11 twice more and Row 10 once more.

Row 17: Maintaining incs made so far, make second dc in a 1 tr and second "ch 2" in "ch 3," work to end of row, rep these incs at end of row.

Rows 18–20: Maintaining all incs, work stitch pattern without shaping to end of row.

Row 21 (inc row): Replace third dc with 1 tr and third "ch 2" in "ch 3," work to end of row, rep incs at end of row.

Row 22: Maintaining all incs, work stitch pattern without shaping to end of row.

Row 23 (inc row): Replace fourth dc with 1 tr and fourth "ch 2" in "ch 3," work to end of row, rep incs at end of row.

Rows 24–26: Maintaining all incs, work stitch pattern without shaping to end of row. Fasten off.

TO FINISH

Arrange the Large Floral Motifs for the Back in nine horizontal rows of 10 large motifs each (see diagram on page 95), arranging them so the petals point north, east, south, and west. Leave a gap of four motifs for the center back neck and place shoulder motifs above the top row as shown. (Note that one shoulder motif on each side is folded in half and shared with the Front.) Arrange the Front in the same way but omit the center two motifs in the ninth row to create the scooped neck. Sew the cardinal points of each neighboring motif together so that south meets north, east meets west, and so on. Once the large motifs of the Front and Back are sewn together, join the motifs of the Back and Front at the shoulders and along the side edges at the same points, leaving the top three motifs unjoined for the sleeve openings. Sew a small floral motif into all the spaces between four large motifs, including along the neck edges; match each of the unattached petals of the surrounding four large motifs to a petal of the small motif leaving the fifth petal of the small motif pointing north unattached. Sew each Sleeve seam and stitch each Sleeve into an armhole opening.

+STRIPED SHIFT DRESS

///

YOU WILL NEED

YARN
4(5:5) x 50g (1¾oz) balls BC Garn *Semilla*, or a similar double-knitting-weight organic wool yarn, in each of three colors:

A dark blue (114)
B mustard (107)
C orange (115)

CROCHET HOOKS
US sizes G/6 and 7 (4mm and 4.5mm) crochet hooks

OTHER EQUIPMENT
Blunt-tipped yarn or tapestry needle, for weaving in yarn ends and sewing seams

GAUGE
3 stars to 4¼in (11cm) and 11 rows to 4in (10cm) measured over stitch pattern using a US size G/6 (4mm) crochet hook.

ABBREVIATIONS
See page 9.

SPECIAL ABBREVIATION
CL (2-dc cluster) = [yo and insert hook in sp/st, yo and draw a loop through, yo and draw through first 2 loops on hook] twice in same sp/st, yo and draw through all 3 loops on hook to complete cluster.
sc2tog = see page 21.
hdc2tog = see page 22.
dc2tog = see page 23.

STRIPE PATTERN
Foundation chain and Rows 1 and 2: Col A.
Rows 3, 4, and 5: Col B.
Rows 6, 7, and 8: Col C.
Cont repeating 3 rows A, 3 rows B, 3 rows C throughout.

STITCH PATTERN
Work patt in rows, turning at end of each row, as follows:
Row 1 (RS): 1 sc in second ch from hook, ch 1, skip 1 ch, 1 sc in next ch, [ch 3, skip 3 ch, 1 sc in next ch] twice, *ch 2, skip 2 ch, 1 sc in next ch, [ch 3, skip 3 ch, 1 sc in next ch] twice; rep from * to last 2 ch, ch 1, skip 1 ch, 1 sc in last ch.
Row 2: Ch 3, in first 1-ch sp work [CL, ch 2, CL], ch 1, skip 1 sc, 1 sc in next sc, *ch 1, skip 3-ch sp, in next 2-ch sp work [CL, (ch 2, CL) 3 times], ch 1, skip 3-ch sp, 1 sc in next sc; rep from * to last 2 sps, ch 1, skip 3-ch sp, in last 1-ch sp work [CL, ch 2, CL], 1 dc in last sc.

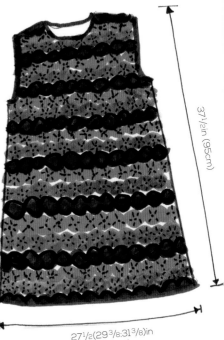

37½in (95cm)

27½(29³/₈:31³/₈)in
70(74.5:79)cm

SIZES

To fit bust (inches)	30–32	34–36	38–40
To fit bust (cm)	76–81	86–91	97–102

FINISHED MEASUREMENTS

Around bust (inches)	36	40	43½
Around bust (cm)	92	101	110
Length (inches)	37½	37½	37½
Length (cm)	95	95	95

Row 3: Ch 1, 1 sc in first dc, *ch 3, work CL in top of each of next 4 CLs, ch 3, 1 sc in next 2-ch sp; rep from * to end placing last sc in top of 3-ch at end of row.

Row 4: Ch 1, 1 sc in first sc, *ch 3, 1 sc in top of next CL, ch 2, skip next 2 CLs, 1 sc in top of next CL, ch 3, 1 sc in next sc; rep from * to end.

Row 5: Ch 1, 1 sc in first sc, *ch 1, skip 3-ch sp, in next 2-ch sp work [CL, (ch 2, CL) 3 times], ch 1, skip 3-ch sp, 1 sc in next sc; rep from * to end.

Row 6: Ch 3, work CL in top of each of next 2 CLs, ch 3, 1 sc in next 2-ch sp, ch 3, *CL in top of each of next 4 CLs, ch 3, 1 sc in next 2-ch sp, ch 3; rep from * to last 2 CLs, work CL in each of last 2 CLs, 1 dc in last sc.

Row 7: Ch 1, 1 sc in first dc, ch 1, skip first CL, 1 sc in next CL, ch 3, 1 sc in next sc, ch 3, *1 sc in top of next CL, ch 2, skip next 2 CLs, 1 sc in top of next CL, ch 3, 1 sc in next sc, ch 3; rep from * to last 2 CLs, 1 sc in next CL, ch 1, skip last CL, 1 sc in top of 3-ch.

Rows 2–7 form stitch pattern.
Rep these rows throughout.

FRONT

Foundation chain: Using a US size 7 (4.5mm) crochet hook and Col A, ch 168(179:190).

Change to a US size G/6 (4mm) crochet hook and cont working in rows, turning at end of each row.

Row 1 (RS): 1 sc in second ch from hook, 1 sc in each of next 6 ch, *ch 3, skip 3 ch, 1 sc in next ch, ch 2, skip 2 ch, 1 sc in next ch, ch 3, skip 3 ch, 1 sc in next ch; rep from * to last 6 ch, 1 sc in each of last 6 ch.

Row 2: Ch 3 (does NOT count as a st), dc2tog over first 2 sc, 1 hdc in each of next 2 sc, 1 sc in next each of next 2 sc, in next sc work stitch pattern Row 5 from first sc, work in patt to last 6 sc, 1 sc in each of next 2 sc, 1 hdc in each of next 2 sc, dc2tog over last 2 sc.

Row 3: Ch 1, 1 dc in top of dc2tog, 1 hdc in each of next 2 hdc, sc2tog over next 2 sc, work stitch pattern Row 6 from first 2-dcCL to last 5 sts, sc2tog over next 2 sc, 1 hdc in each of next 2 hdc, 1 dc in top of dc2tog at end.

Row 4: 1 sc in each of next first 4 sts, ch 1, work stitch pattern Row 7 from second sc to last 4 sts, ch 1, 1 sc in each of last 4 sts.

Row 5: Ch 3, 1 dc in first st, hdc2tog of next 2 sts, 1 sc in next st, work stitch pattern Row 2 to last 4 sts, 1 sc in next st, hdc2tog over next 2 sts, 1 dc in last st.

Row 6: Ch 3, work 1 dc and 1 hdc tog over first 2 sts, 1 sc in next st, work stitch pattern Row 3 to last 3 sts, 1 sc in next st, work 1 hdc and 1 dc tog over last 2 sts.

Row 7: Ch 1, 1 sc in each of first 2 sts, work stitch pattern Row 4 to last 2 sts, 1 sc in each of last 2 sts.

Row 8: Ch 3, work 1 dc and 1 hdc tog over first 2 sts, work stitch pattern Row 5 to last 2 sts, work 1 hdc and 1 dc tog over last 2 sts.

Row 9: Ch 3, [2 dc, 2 hdc, 1 sc, sc2tog] over top of first half star, work stitch pattern Row 6 to last half star, [sc2tog, 1 sc, 2 hdc, 2 dc] over last half star.

Row 10: Ch 1, 1 sc in each of first 6 sts, work stitch pattern Row 7 to last 6 sts, 1 sc in each of last 6 sts.
Rep Rows 2–10 until a total of 64 rows have been worked from beg, ending with Col A. (You now have 20 star rows and 2 half star rows at beg and end.)
Starting with stitch pattern Row 5, cont working 15 rows in stitch patt with no variation from instructions (no decs). Fasten off.

SHAPE ARMHOLE
Keeping stripe sequence correct, rejoin yarn at side edge.

Row 1: Skip one star (join in center of star), work stitch pattern Row 2 to center of last full star, turn.

Row 2: Work stitch pattern Row 3, turn.

Row 3: Work stitch pattern Row 4, turn.

Row 4: Ch 4, skip 3-ch space and 1 dc, work stitch pattern Row 2, replacing "ch 3" with 1 dc in 2-ch sp and leaving last 1 dc and 3-ch space unworked, turn.***

SHAPE NECK
Leaving 3(4:5) stars unworked in center front, work each side of neck separately, starting at armhole edge.
Cont working in stitch pattern, starting with a stitch pattern Row 3, for 12 rows more and AT THE SAME TIME dec by one dc2tog on the first and every foll third row (stitch pattern rows: 3, 6, 3, 6).

SHAPE SHOULDER
Cont working in stitch pattern for 2 rows more.
Work a final row but exchanging all sts for sc over first star and for hdc over second star to create a slope.
Fasten off.
Rejoin yarn to other side edge and rep neck and armhole shaping, reversing all shaping.

BACK

Work as given for Front to ***.
Work 9 rows more in stitch pattern without shaping.

SHAPE NECK
Work each side of neck separately.
Starting at side edge, work 3 rows more in stitch pattern, leaving center three stars unworked.
Work shoulder shaping as given for Front.

TO FINISH

Weave in any loose yarn ends to the back of your work so that they are not visible from the right side.
Sew together the Front and Back at the shoulders.
Sew the side seams, carefully matching the stripes.

FAN STITCH CARDIGAN

///

YOU WILL NEED

YARN
9(11) x 50g (1¾oz) balls of BC Garn *Semilla Grosso*, or a similar bulky-weight organic wool yarn, in bright pink (123)

OTHER MATERIALS
Five ⅞in (2cm) buttons

CROCHET HOOK
US size J/10 (6mm) crochet hook

OTHER EQUIPMENT
Blunt-tipped yarn or tapestry needle, for weaving in yarn ends and sewing seams

GAUGE
One full pattern repeat measures approximately 2⅜in (6cm) wide and 2½in (6.5cm) tall using a US size J/10 (6mm) crochet hook.

ABBREVIATIONS
See page 9.

SIZES

To fit bust (inches)	Up to 36	Up to 44
To fit bust (cm)	Up to 91	Up to 112

FINISHED MEASUREMENTS

Around bust (inches)	36½	43½
Around bust (cm)	92	110
Length (inches)	19¾	19¾
Length (cm)	50	50
Sleeve seam (inches)	8½	8½
Sleeve seam (cm)	22	22

FAN STITCH PATTERN IN SYMBOLS
See page 9 for symbols.

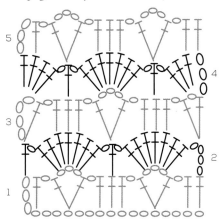

BACK

Foundation chain: Using a US size J/10 (6mm) crochet hook, ch 59(67).

Beg stitch pattern and work in rows, turning at end of each row, as follows:

Row 1 (WS): 1 dc in fourth ch from hook, *ch 1, skip 2 ch, in next ch work [1 dc, ch 3, 1 dc—called a V-st], ch 1, skip 2 ch, 1 dc in each of next 3 ch; rep from * to end omitting 1 dc at end of last rep.

Row 2: Ch 4 (counts as first dc and 1-ch), work 7 dc in next 3-ch sp, ch 1, skip 2 dc, 1 dc in next dc, *ch 1, 7 dc in next 3-ch sp , ch 1, skip 2 dc, 1 dc in next dc; rep from * working last dc of last rep in top of 3-ch.

Row 3: Ch 4 (counts as first dc and 1-ch), 1 dc in first dc, ch 1, skip 2 dc, 1 dc in each of next 3 dc, *ch 1, skip 2 dc, in next dc work [1 dc, ch 3, 1 dc], ch 1, skip 2 dc, 1 dc in each of next 3 dc; rep from * to last 2 dc, skip 2 dc, in third of 4-ch at beg of previous row work [1 dc, ch 1, 1 dc].

Row 4: Ch 3 (counts as first dc), 3 dc in first 1-ch sp, ch 1, skip 2 dc, 1 dc in next dc, *ch 1, 7 dc in next 3-ch sp, ch 1, skip 2 dc, 1 dc in next dc; rep from * to last 2 dc, ch 1, skip 2 dc, 3 dc in last ch sp (sp created by tch) 1 dc in third of 4-ch at beg of previous row.

Row 5: Ch 3 (counts as first dc), skip first dc, 1 dc in next dc, *ch 1, skip 2 dc, in next dc work [1 dc, ch 3, 1 dc], ch 1, skip 2 dc, 1 dc in each of next 3 dc; rep from * to end omitting 1 dc at end of last rep and working last dc in third of 3-ch at beg of previous row.

[Rep Rows 2–5] 4 times more.**

SHAPE ARMHOLE

Row 1 (RS): Work as Row 2 of stitch pattern: sl st to first dc of first V-st, ch 3 (counts as first dc), 1 dc in second arm of V-st, work in patt to last V-st of row, 1 dc in first arm of V-st, 1 dc in second arm of V-st, turn.

Row 2: Work as Row 3 of stitch pattern: ch 3 (counts as first dc), V-st in dc between two 1-ch sps, work in stitch pattern to end of row, ending after last V-st, 1 dc in top of 3-ch of previous row, turn.

Row 3: Work as Row 4 of stitch pattern: ch 3 (counts as first dc), 3 dc in 3-ch space, work in stitch pattern to last 3-ch sp, 3 dc in 3-ch sp, 1 dc in top of 3-ch of previous row, turn.

Row 4: Work as Row 5 of stitch pattern.

Rep Rows 2–5 of stitch pattern twice more then rep Rows 2–3 once more.

Fasten off.

LEFT FRONT

Foundation chain: Using a US size J/10 (6mm) crochet hook, ch 35(43).

Work as for Back to **.

SHAPE ARMHOLE

Row 1 (RS): Work as Row 2 of stitch pattern: sl st to first arm of first V-st, ch 3 (counts as first dc), 1 dc in second arm of V-st, work in stitch pattern to end of row, turn.

Row 2: Work as Row 3 of stitch pattern: work in stitch pattern to end of row, ending after last V-st, 1 dc in top of 3-ch of previous row, turn.

Row 3: Work as Row 4 of stitch pattern: ch 3, 3 dc in 3-ch sp, work in stitch pattern to end of row, turn.

Row 4: Work as Row 5 of stitch pattern.

51/2in (14cm)

61/4in (16cm)

193/4in (50cm)

81/2in (22cm)

181/4(213/4)in
46(55)cm

SHAPE NECK

Row 1 (RS): Work as Row 2 of stitch pattern: work in stitch pattern to last V-st, 1 dc in first arm of V-st, turn.

Row 2: Work as Row 3: ch 3, skip 1 st, 2 dc in next dc, work in stitch pattern to end of row, turn.

Row 3: Work as Row 4: work in stitch pattern to last 2 dc, 1 dc in next dc, skip 1 dc, 1 dc in top of tch, turn.

Row 4: Work as Row 5: ch 3, work V-st in 1 dc between two 1-ch sps, work in stitch pattern to end of row, turn.

Row 5: Work as Row 2: work in stitch pattern to last 3-ch sp of last V-st, 3 dc in 3-ch sp, 1 dc in top of tch, turn.

Row 6: Work as Row 3: ch 3, 1 dc in center st of 3-dc group, work in stitch pattern to end of row, turn.

Row 7: Work as Row 4: work in stitch pattern to last 3-ch sp of last V-st, 7 dc in 3-ch sp, ch 1, 1 dc in top of tch, turn.

Row 8: Ch 4, 1 dc in first dc, work in stitch pattern to end of row, turn.

Rows 9–10: Work in stitch pattern as set. Fasten off.

RIGHT FRONT

Foundation chain: Using a US size J/10 (6mm) crochet hook, ch 35(43).

Work as for Back to **.

SHAPE ARMHOLE

Row 1 (RS): Work as Row 2 of stitch pattern: work in stitch pattern to last V-st of row, 1 dc in first arm of V-st, 1 dc in second arm, turn.

Row 2: Work as Row 3 of stitch pattern: ch 3 (counts as first dc), V-st in dc between two 1-ch sps, work in stitch pattern to end of row, turn.

Row 3: Work as Row 4 of stitch pattern: work in stitch pattern to last 3-ch sp, 3 dc in 3-ch sp, 1 dc in top of 3-ch of previous row, turn.

Row 4: Work as Row 5 of stitch pattern.

SHAPE NECK

Row 1 (RS): Work as Row 2 of stitch pattern: sl st to second arm of first V-st, ch 4, 1 dc in center st of 3 dc, work in stitch pattern to end of row, turn.

Row 2: Work as Row 3: work to last dc, 2 dc in next dc, 1 dc in top of tch, turn.

Row 3: Work as Row 4: ch 4, 1 dc in third dc, ch 1, 1 dc in center st of 3-dc group, work in stitch pattern to end of row, turn.

Row 4: Work as Row 5: work to last V-st of row, work V-st, work 1 dc in top of tch, turn.

Row 5: Work as Row 2: ch 3, 3 dc in 3-ch sp of first V-st, work in stitch pattern to end of row, turn.

Row 6: Work as Row 3: work to last V-st of row, work V-st, ch 1, 1 dc in center st of 3-dc group, 1 dc in top of tch, turn.

Row 7: Work as Row 4: ch 4, 7 dc in 3-ch sp, work in stitch pattern to end of row.

Rows 8–10: Work in stitch pattern as set. Fasten off.

SLEEVES (MAKE 2)

Foundation chain: Using a US size J/10 (6mm) crochet hook, ch 43(51).

Work Rows 1–5 of stitch pattern as given for Back.

Work Rows 2–5 as given for Back 3 times more.

SHAPE SLEEVE CAP

Row 1 (RS): Work as Row 2 of stitch pattern: sl st to second arm of first V-st, ch 4, 1 dc in center st of 3-dc group, work in patt to last V-st of previous row, 1 dc in first arm of V-st, turn.

Row 2: Work as Row 3 of stitch pattern: ch 3, skip first dc, work V-st in next dc, work in patt to last dc, V-st in last dc, 1 dc in top of tch, turn.

Row 3: Work as Row 4 of stitch pattern: ch 3, 3 dc in 3-ch sp, work in patt to last 3-ch sp, 3 dc in 3-ch sp, 1 dc in top of tch, turn.

Row 4: Work as Row 5 of stitch pattern: ch 4, work V-st in next dc between two 1-ch sps, work in patt to last V-st, work V-st, ch 1, 1 dc in top of tch, turn.

Row 5: Work as Row 2 of stitch pattern: 3ch, 3 dc in 3-ch sp, work in patt to last 3-ch sp, 3 dc in last 3-ch sp, 1 dc in top of tch, turn.

Row 6: Work as Row 3 of stitch pattern: ch 4, work V-st in next dc between two 1-ch sps, work in patt to last V-st, work V-st, ch 1, 1 dc in top of tch, turn.

Row 7: Work as Row 4 of stitch pattern: ch 3, 2 dc in 3-ch sp, work in patt to last 3-ch sp, 2 dc in last 3-ch sp, 1 dc in top of tch.

Row 8: Work as Row 5 of stitch pattern: ch 3, skip first 2 dc, 1 dc in next dc, work in patt to last 2 dc, 1 dc in next dc, skip 1 dc, 1 dc in top of tch.
Fasten off.

PATCH POCKETS (MAKE 2)

Foundation row: Using a US size J/10 (6mm) crochet hook, ch 19.
Work Rows 1–5 of stitch pattern as given for Back.
Work Rows 2–3 as given for Back.
Fasten off.

TO FINISH

Weave in any loose ends into the back of your work so they are not visible from the RS.

Begin by sewing together the shoulder seams, then pin the Sleeve caps into the armholes and sew them in place. Finally, stitch up the side seams by sewing the Fronts and Back together up to the underarm, then stitch up along the Sleeve. Stitch on your patch pockets.

Work the edgings that follow with a US size J/10 (6mm) crochet hook.

ADD NECK EDGING

With RS facing, join yarn to beg of neck edge on Right Front, ch 3, work dc evenly all the way around to center front edge of Left Front.
Fasten off.

ADD BUTTON BAND TO LEFT FRONT

With RS facing, rejoin yarn to top front edge of Left Front, ch 3, work dc evenly all the way down front edge, turn.
Cont working in rows, turning at end of each row.
Next row (WS): Ch 1, 1 sc in each st to end of row.
Next row: Ch 3, 1 dc in each st to end of row.
Fasten off.

ADD BUTTONHOLE BAND TO RIGHT FRONT

On Right Front place markers at your preferred positions for the five buttonholes so you can work them in the correct places.
With RS facing, rejoin yarn to bottom front edge of Right Front, ch 3, work dc evenly all the way up front edge, turn.
Cont working in rows, turning at end of each row.
Next row (WS): Ch 1, *1 sc in each st to next button marker, ch 1, skip 1 st; rep from * to last marker, 1 sc in each st to end of row.
Next row: Ch 3, 1 dc in each st to end of row.
Fasten off.
Sew buttons on Left Front button band to match buttonholes on Right Front.

DAISY SWING COAT

///

YOU WILL NEED

YARN
Wool And The Gang *Shiny Happy Cotton*, or a similar Aran-weight cotton yarn, in three colors:

A 12(12:12:13:13:13) x 100g (3½oz) balls in bright blue (True Blue)

B 1(1:1:1:1:1) x 100g (3½oz) ball in bright yellow (Yellow Brick Road)

C 1(1:1:1:1:1) x 100g (3½oz) ball in white (White Noise)

CROCHET HOOK
US size H/8 (5mm) crochet hook

OTHER EQUIPMENT
Blunt-tipped yarn or tapestry needle, for weaving in yarn ends and sewing seams

GAUGE
18 sts and 22 rows to 4in (10cm) measured over single crochet using a US size H/8 (5mm) crochet hook.

ABBREVIATIONS
See page 9.

SPECIAL ABBREVIATION
sc2tog = [insert hook in next st, yo and draw a loop through] twice (3 loops now on hook), yo and draw through all 3 loops on hook to decrease one stitch.

SIZES

To fit bust (inches)	30	32	34	36	38	40
To fit bust (cm)	76	81	86	91	97	102

FINISHED MEASUREMENTS

Around bust (inches)	32	34	35½	38	40	42½
Around bust (cm)	80	84	89	96	100	106
Length (inches)	23½	23½	24	24½	24¾	25
Length (cm)	60	60	61	62	63	64
Sleeve seam (inches)	12½	12½	12½	13	1.3	13¼
Sleeve seam (cm)	32	32	32	33	33	34

23½(23½:24:24½:24¾:25)in
60(60:61:62:63:64)cm

12½(12½:12½:13:13:13¼)in
32(32:32:33:33:34)cm

24½(25¼:26¼:27½:28½:29¾)in
61(63:65.5:69:71:74.5)cm

BACK

Foundation chain: Using a US size H/8 (5mm) crochet hook and Col A, ch 111(115:119:125:129:135).

Cont working in rows, turning at end of each row.

Row 1: 1 sc in second ch from hook, 1 sc in each ch to end of row. *110(114:118:124:128:134) sc.*

Row 2: Ch 1 (does NOT count as a st), 1 sc in each st to end of row.

Rows 3–10: Work 8 rows as Row 2.

Bust sizes 38in (97cm) and 40in (102cm) only

Rep Row 2 twice more.

All sizes

Row 1: Ch 1, work dec by working next 2 sts tog (sc2tog), 1 sc in each st to last 3 sts, sc2tog, 1 sc in last st. *108(112:116:122:126:132) sts.*

Row 2: Ch 1, 1 sc in each st to end of row.

Rows 3–4: Work as Row 2.

Rep these 4 rows 18 times more. *72(76:80:86:90:96) sts.*

SHAPE ARMHOLE

Row 1: Ch 1, 1 sc in each st to last 4(4:4:5:5:6) sts, turn.

Row 2: Work as Row 1. *64(68:72:76:80:84) sts.*

Row 3: Ch 1, sc2tog, 1 sc in each st to last 3 sts, sc2tog, 1 sc in last st. *62(66:70:74:78:82) sts.*

Row 4: Ch 1, 1 sc in each st to end of row.

[Rep Rows 3–4] 4(4:4:5:5:6) times more. *54(58:62:64:68:70) sts.*

Cont repeating Row 4 only, working even in sc without any further shaping, until work measures 23½(23½:24:24½:24¾:25)in/60(60:61:62:63:64)cm.

SHAPE SHOULDER

Row 1: Ch 1, 1 sl st in each of first 6(7:8:8:8:9) sts, 1 sc in each st to last 6(7:8:8:8:9) sts, turn.

Row 2: Ch 1, 1 sl st in each of first 5(6:7:7:8:8) sts, 1 sc in each st to last 5(6:7:7:8:8) sts.

Fasten off.

LEFT FRONT

Foundation chain: Using a US size H/8 (5mm) crochet hook and Col A, ch 63(65:67:70:72:75).

Cont working in rows, turning at end of each row.

Row 1: 1 sc in second ch from hook, 1 sc in each ch to end. *62(64:66:69:71:74) sc.*

Row 2: Ch 1 (does NOT count as a st), 1 sc in each st to end of row.

Rows 3–10: Work 8 rows as Row 2.

Bust sizes 38in (97cm) and 40in (102cm) only

Rep Row 2 twice more.

All sizes

Row 1: Ch 1, sc2tog, 1 sc in each st to end of row. *61(63:65:68:70:73) sts.*

Row 2: Ch 1, 1 sc in each st to end of row.

Rows 3–4: Work as Row 2.

Rep these 4 rows 18 times more. *43(45:47:50:52:55) sts.*

SHAPE ARMHOLE

Row 1: Ch 1, 1 sc in each st to end of row.

Row 2: Ch 1, 1 sc in each st to last 4(4:5:5:6) sts, turn. *39(41:43:45:47:49) sts.*

Row 3: Ch 1, sc2tog, 1 sc in each st to end of row. *38(40:42:44:46:48) sts.*

Row 4: Ch 1, 1 sc in each st to end of row.

[Rep Rows 3–4] 4(4:4:5:5:6) times more. *34(36:38:39:41:42) sts.*

Cont working even in sc, without shaping, until work measures 21¼in (54cm), ending with a WS row.

SHAPE NECK

Row 1 (RS): Ch 1, 1 sc in each st until 16 sts rem, turn.

Row 2: Ch 1, sc2tog, 1 sc in each st to end of row.

Row 3: Ch 1, 1 sc in each st until 3 sts rem, sc2tog, 1 sc in last st.

Row 4: Work as Row 2.

Row 5: Work as Row 3.

Row 6: Work as Row 2.

Row 7: Work as Row 3.

Row 8: Work as Row 2.

Cont working even in sc without shaping, until work measures 23½(23½:24:24½:24¾:25)in/60(60:61:62:63:64)cm or same as Back.

SHAPE SHOULDER

Row 1: Ch 1, 1 sl st in each of first 6(7:8:8:8:9) sts, 1 sc in each st to end of row.

Row 2: Ch 1, 1 sc in each of first 4(5:6:6:7:7) sts.

Fasten off.

RIGHT FRONT

Work as given for Left Front, but working three WS buttonhole rows when work measures 11¾in (30cm), 15¾in (40cm), and 19¾in (50cm) as follows:

Buttonhole row (WS): Ch 1, then working toward center front, work 1 sc in each st to last 8 sts, ch 3, skip 3 sts, 1 sc in each of next 5 sts.

When working next row, work 1 sc in each st including in each of 3-ch of buttonhole.

Cont working Right Front as given for Left Front.

SLEEVES (MAKE 2)

Foundation chain: Using a US size H/8 (5mm) crochet hook and Col A, ch 59(59:61:61:63:65).

Cont working in rows, turning at end of each row.

Row 1: 1 sc in second ch from hook, 1 sc in each ch to end of row. *58(58:60:60:62:64) sc.*

Row 2: Ch 1 (does NOT count as a st), 1 sc in each sc to end of row.

Rep Row 2 until work measures 12½(12½:12½:13:13: 13¼)in/32(32:32:33:33:34)cm.

SHAPE SLEEVE CAPS

Row 1: Ch 1, 1 sc in each st to last 4 sts, turn.

Row 2: Work as Row 1. *50(50:52:52:54:56) sts.*

Work dec rows as follows:

Row 3: Ch 1, sc2tog, 1 sc in each st until last 3 sts, sc2tog, 1 sc in last st, turn.

Row 4: Ch 1, 1 sc in each st to end of row.

[Rep Rows 3–4] 16(16:16:16:17:17) times more. Fasten off.

BUTTONHOLE FLOWERS (MAKE 3)

Foundation ring: Using a US size H/8 (5mm) crochet hook and Col C, ch 7 and join with a sl st in first ch to form a ring.

Cont working in rounds, with RS always facing.

Round 1 (RS): Ch 1, 20 sc in center of ring, join with a sl st in top of first sc.

Round 2 (petals): *Ch 3, [yo twice, insert hook in next sc, yo and draw a loop through, (yo and draw through first 2 loops on hook) twice] 3 times (4 loops now on hook), yo and draw through all 4 loops on hook, cut off yarn and fasten off**, then rejoin yarn in next sc; rep from * 4 times more around ring, ending last rep at **. *5 petals.*

BUTTONS (MAKE 3)

Foundation ring: Using a US size H/8 (5mm) crochet hook and Col B, make a loose slip knot.

Cont working in rounds, with RS always facing.

Round 1 (RS): Ch 1, 3 sc in slip knot, join with sl st in top of 1-ch and pull slip knot tight. *3 sc.*

Round 2: Ch 1, 2 sc in each sc, join with a sl st in top of 1-ch. *6 sc.*

Round 3: Ch 1, 1 sc in each sc, join with a sl st in top of 1-ch.

Row 3: Ch 1, [sc2tog] 3 times, join with a sl st in top of 1-ch. *3 sc.*

Fasten off, leaving a long yarn tail.

Using a blunt-tipped yarn or tapestry needle and long yarn tail, gather stitches of last row together to form a ball shape.

TO FINISH

Weave in any yarn ends into the wrong side of the fabric so that they are not visible from the right side.

Begin by sewing the shoulder seams together, then pin the Sleeve caps into the armholes of the Front and Back pieces, and stitch them in place. Finally, sew up the side seams by stitching from the bottom of the garment up to the armhole and then all along the Sleeve seam.

Stitch buttonhole flowers onto the Right Front, positioning one around the opening of each buttonhole. Sew the buttons onto the Left Front to match the buttonholes on Right Front.

ADD EDGING

Using a US size H/8 (5mm) crochet hook and your preferred color—either the main color or a contrasting shade—add an edging around the edge of your jacket as follows:

With RS facing, join yarn at beg of bottom edge of Back, ch 3, 2 dc at base of 3-ch, *3 dc in space about ¾in (2cm) along; rep from * along bottom edge of garment, work 5 dc in corner, cont up center front, work 5 dc in corner, cont around neck, work 5 dc in corner, cont down center front, work 5 dc in corner, cont along bottom of garment to meet first 3-ch, join with sl st in top of 3-ch.

Repeat edging around Sleeve edges.

ENLARGED GRANNY SQUARE SWEATER

//

YOU WILL NEED

YARN
Debbie Bliss *Rialto DK*, or a similar double-knitting-weight wool yarn, in four colors:
A 7 x 50g (1¾oz) balls in dark purple (62 Mulberry)
B 2 x 50g (1¾oz) balls in mauve (64 Mauve)
C 2 x 50g (1¾oz) balls in coral pink (55 Coral)
D 2 x 50g (1¾oz) balls in pale blue (60 Sky)

CROCHET HOOK
US size G/6 (4mm) crochet hook

OTHER EQUIPMENT
Blunt-tipped yarn or tapestry needle, for weaving in yarn ends and sewing seams

GAUGE
5½ repeats of 3-dc cluster and 12 rows to 4in (10cm) measured over stitch pattern using a US size G/6 (4mm) crochet hook.

ABBREVIATIONS
See page 9.

SIZES

To fit bust (inches)	32	34	36	38	40
To fit bust (cm)	81	86	91	97	102

FINISHED MEASUREMENTS

Around bust (inches)	40½	42	43½	45	46½
Around bust (cm)	102	106	109	113	116
Length (inches)	19¾	20½	21¼	22	22¾
Length (cm)	50	52	54	56	58
Sleeve seam (inches)	17¾	17¾	17¾	17¾	17¾
Sleeve seam (cm)	45	45	45	45	45

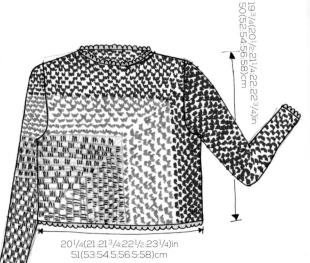

19¾(20½:21¼:22:22¾)in
50(52:54:56:58)cm

20¼(21:21¾:22½:23¼)in
51(53:54.5:56.5:58)cm

+GRANNY SQUARES

MAKING A GRANNY SQUARE

Choose four colors (Cols A, B, C, and D).

Foundation ring: Using Col A, ch 4 and join with a sl st in first ch to form a ring.

Round 1: Ch 3 (counts as 1 dc), 2 dc in ring, ch 2 (corner), *3 dc in ring, ch 2 (corner); rep from * twice more, join with a sl st in top of 3-ch. Fasten off.

Round 2: Join Col B in a corner 2-ch sp, ch 3, [2 dc, ch 2, 3 dc] in same sp, ch 1, *[3 dc, ch 2, 3 dc] in next 2-ch sp, ch 1; rep from * twice more, join a with a sl st in top of 3-ch. Fasten off.

Round 3: Join Col C in a corner 2-ch sp, ch 3, [2 dc, ch 2, 3 dc] in same sp, ch 1, 3 dc in next 1-ch sp, ch 1, *[3 dc, ch 2, 3 dc] in next 2-ch sp, ch 1, 3 dc in next 1-ch sp, ch 1; rep from * twice more, join a with a sl st in top of 3-ch. Fasten off.

Round 4: Join Col D in a corner 2-ch sp, ch 3, [2 dc, ch 2, 3 dc] in same sp, ch 1, [3 dc in next 1-ch sp, ch 1] twice, *[3 dc, ch 2, 3 dc] in next 2-ch sp, ch 1, [3 dc in next 1-ch sp, ch 1] twice; rep from * twice more, join a with a sl st in top of 3-ch. Fasten off.

CROCHETING TOGETHER GRANNY SQUARES

To join your granny squares together you can simply sew them together using the mattress stitch method or you can crochet them together. To crochet them together, hold two granny squares with wrong sides together.

Step 1 Work sc along the edge but crochet through stitches on both granny squares as you work, joining the two squares together.

Step 2 The seam will look like this on the wrong side of your work.

Step 3 And the seam will look like this on the right side of your work.

BACK

Foundation chain: Using a US size G/6 (4mm) crochet hook and Col A, ch 115(119:123:127:131).

Cont working in rows, turning at end of each row.

Row 1 (RS): 1 dc in fourth ch from hook, *ch 1, skip 1 ch, 1 dc in each of next 3 ch; rep from * to last 3 ch, ch 1, skip 1 ch, 1 dc in each of last 2 ch.

Row 2: Ch 4 (counts as 1 dc and 1-ch sp), *3 dc in next 1-ch sp, ch 1; rep from * to end, ending with 1 dc in top of tch.

Row 3: Ch 3, 1 dc in first 1-ch sp, ch 1, *3 dc in next 1-ch sp, ch 1; rep from * to last sp at edge, 1 dc in last sp, 1 dc in third of 4-ch of previous row.

Rep Rows 2–3 until work measures 9½(10¼:11:11⅞:12½)in/24(26:28:30:32)cm, ending with a WS row.

SHAPE ARMHOLE

Row 1 (RS): Ch 1, sl st 6 sts across 2 groups of 3-dc; work in patt until 2 groups of 3-dc rem, turn.

Row 2: Work in patt to end.

Rows 3–8: Ch 3, skip 2 sts, work in patt to end of row.

Cont working in patt without shaping until work measures 19(19¾:20½:21¼:22)in/48(50:52:54:56)cm.

SHAPE SHOULDER

Row 1 (RS): Ch 1, 1 sl st in each of first 4(6:8:10:12) sts across 1(1½:2:2½:3) groups of 3-dc; work in patt until 1(1½:2:2½:3) groups of 3-dc rem, turn.

Rows 2–3: Work in patt to end to row.

Fasten off.

FRONT

Foundation ring: Using a US size G/6 (4mm) crochet hook and Col B, ch 4 and join with a sl st in first ch to form a ring.

Cont working in rows, turning at end of each row.

Row 1 (RS): Ch 3 (counts as first dc on all RS rows), 2 dc in ring, ch 2, 3 dc in ring.

Row 2: Ch 4 (counts as 1 dc and 1-ch sp on all WS rows), [3 dc, ch 2, 3 dc] in 2-ch sp, ch 1, 1 dc in top of 3-ch.

Row 3: Ch 3, 2 dc in first 1-ch sp, ch 1, [3 dc, ch 2 (corner), 3 dc] in 2-ch sp, ch 1, 3 dc in last 1-ch sp (formed by 4-ch).

Row 4: Ch 4, 3 dc in first 1-ch sp, ch 1, [3 dc, ch 2, 3 dc] in corner sp, ch 1, 3 dc in next 1-ch sp, ch 1, 1 dc in top of tch.

Row 5: Ch 3, 2 dc in first 1-ch sp, ch 1, 3 dc in next 1-ch sp, ch 1, [3 dc, ch 2, 3 dc] in corner space, ch 1, 3 dc in next 1-ch sp, ch 1, 2 dc in last 1-ch sp.

Cont working in granny square st patt enlarging square as set by Rows 4 and 5 until square measures 4¾(5⅛:5½:6:6¼)in/12(13:14:15:16)cm.

Change to Col C and cont working in granny square st patt as set until square measures 9⅜(10¼:11:11⅞:12½)in/24(26:28:30:32)cm, ending with a WS row.

SHAPE ARMHOLE

Change to Col D.

Row 1 (RS): Work until 2 groups of 3-dc rem, 1 dc in center of next 3-dc group, turn.

Row 2: Work in patt to end of row.

Row 3: Work in patt to last 3-dc group, 2 dc in next ch sp, turn.

Row 4: Ch 3, 1 dc in next ch sp, work in patt to end of row.

Rep Rows 3 and 4 twice more.

Cont working in granny square st patt as set without shaping until square measures 14⅛(15⅜:16½:17¾:18⅞)in/36(39:42:45:48)cm.

Change to Col A and cont working in granny square st patt as set until square measures 14⅞(16½:17¼:18⅛:18⅞)in/40(42:44:46:48)cm , ending with a WS row.

SHAPE NECK

Cont with Col A only.

Row 1 (RS): Work around square until 9(9⅜:9⅞:10¼:10⅝)in/23(24:25:26:27)cm rem of row along top edge, turn.

Row 2: Work back around to end of row. Fasten off. Leaving a gap of 4⅝in (12cm) for neck opening, place a marker at each end.

With RS facing, rejoin Col A at side edge and work each side of neck separately.

Bust sizes 32in (81cm), 36in (91cm), and 40in (102cm) only

Row 1 (RS): Ch 3, 1 dc in corner sp of square, work in patt for 5(–:6:–:7) 3-dc groups, 2 dc in next sp, turn.

Row 2: Ch 3, 3 dc in next sp, work in patt to end of row.

Bust sizes 34in (86cm) and 38in (97cm) only

Row 1 (RS): Ch 3, 1 dc in corner sp of square, work in patt for –(6:–:7:–) 3-dc groups, turn.

Row 2: Ch 3, 3 dc in next sp , work in patt to end of row.

All sizes

Row 3: Ch 3, 1 dc in corner sp of square, work in patt for 4(5:5:6:6) 3-dc groups, turn.

Row 4: Ch 3, 3 dc in next sp, work in patt to end of row.

Row 5: Ch 3, 1 dc in corner sp of square, work in patt for 3(4:4:5:5) 3-dc groups, turn.

Row 6: Ch 3, 2 dc in next sp, ch 1, 3 dc in next 1(1:2:2:3) ch sps, ch 1, 2 dc in next sp , turn.

Row 7: Ch 3, 3 dc in next 1(1:2:2:3) ch sps, ch 1, 1 dc in next sp.

Fasten off.

With RS facing, rejoin yarn at other side edge.

Row 1: Ch 3, work in patt to shoulder edge.
Rows 2–3: Work in patt as set to end of row.
Rows 4–10: Work as Rows 1–7 as given for previous side of neck.

SHAPE LEFT SIDE EDGE OF FRONT

Match this to the other side edge of the Front. It's quite tricky to get perfect as you're crocheting in a different direction.
With RS facing, rejoin Col A yarn at bottom of work.
Row 1: Ch 3, work approximately 11(11⅞:12 6/8:13⅜:14⅛:15)in/28(30:32:34:36:38)cm of patt, matching other edge, turn.
Row 2: Work in patt to end of row.
Row 3: Work as Row 1 for approximately 9⅞(10⅝:11½:12⅛:13)in/25(27:29:31:33)cm, turn.
Row 4: Work as Row 2.
Row 5: Work as Row 1 for 8⅝(9½:10¼:11:11⅞)in/22(24:26:28:30)cm, turn.
Row 6: Work as Row 2.
Rows 7–10: Work in patt without shaping.
Fasten off.

PLAIN SLEEVE (MAKE 1)

Foundation chain: Using a US size G/6 (4mm) crochet hook and Col A, ch 51(51:55:55:59).
Row 1: 1 dc in fourth ch from hook, *ch 1, skip 1 ch, 1 dc in each of next 3 ch; rep from * to last 3 ch, ch 1, skip 1 ch, 1 dc in each of last 2 ch.
Row 2: Ch 4 (counts as 1 dc and 1-ch sp), *3 dc in next 1-ch sp, ch 1; rep from * to end, ending with 1 dc in top of tch.
Row 3: Ch 3, 1 dc in first 1-ch sp, ch 1, *3 dc in next 1-ch sp, ch 1; rep from * to last sp at edge, 1 dc in last sp, 1 dc in third of 4-ch of previous row.
Rep Rows 2–3 until until work measures approximately 2¼in (6cm), ending with a patt Row 2.
Inc row 1 (RS): Ch 3, 2 dc in first 1-ch sp, *3 dc in next 1-ch sp, ch 1; rep from * to end of row, ending with 3 dc in last sp, turn.
Inc row 2 (WS): Ch 3, 1 dc in first dc, ch 1, *3 dc in next 1-ch sp, ch 1; rep from * to end of row, ending with 2 dc in top of tch.
Beg with a patt Row 2, cont working in patt as set until work measures approximately 4⅝in (12cm), ending with a patt Row 2.
Note number of rows worked from last inc row.
Work Inc Rows 1–2 once more.
***Working inc rows at regular intervals, beg with a patt Row 2 and cont working in patt as set until same number of rows have been worked as between pairs of inc rows, ending with a patt Row 2.
Work Inc Rows 1–2 once more.
Rep from *** 4 times more.
Cont working in granny square stitch pattern without shaping until Sleeve measures 17¾in (45cm) from foundation-chain edge.
Fasten off.

SHAPE SLEEVE CAP

Row 1 (RS): Skip 2 reps, rejoin yarn to center dc of next 3-dc group, ch 3, work to same point at other end of row, turn.
Row 2: Work in patt as set.
Row 3: Ch 4, skip first group of either 2-dc or 3-dc, work in patt, skip last group, 1 dc in top of tch.
Row 4: Work in patt as set to end of row.
[Rep Rows 3–4] 8 times more.
Rep Row 3 once more.
Fasten off.

STRIPED SLEEVE (MAKE 1)

Work as given for Plain Sleeve, but using Col B until work measures 13in (33cm).
Change to Col C and cont until work measures 18¼in (46.5cm) or stripe is equal to depth of Col C stripe on Front.
Change to Col D and cont until work measures 23⅝in (60cm) or stripe is equal to depth of Col C stripe on Front.
Change to Col A and cont until Sleeve has been completed.

TO FINISH

Weave in any yarn ends into the wrong side of the fabric so that they are not visible from the right side.
Lightly steam each garment piece before sewing together.
Sew together the Back and Fronts at the shoulders.
Pin the Sleeve caps into the armholes to make sure the garment pieces don't slip around and change position, then sew in place.
Sew up the side seams all the way from the bottom of the garment up to the underarm and along the Sleeve seam.

ADD EDGING

Add the edging around the cuffs, neckline, and bottom of sweater using Col C as follows:
Join Col C to one of the 1-ch sps between two 3-dc groups at the back of the garment, ch 3, work 2 dc in same sp, *3 dc in next 1-ch sp, ch 1; rep from * all the way around, join with a sl st in top of 3-ch.

PATCHWORK STITCH SWEATER

YOU WILL NEED

YARN
6(7:8) x 100g (3½oz) hanks of Ginger's Hand Dyed *Sheepish DK*, or a similar double-knitting-weight wool yarn, in pale pink (Barbapapa)

CROCHET HOOK
US size 7 (4.5mm) crochet hook

OTHER EQUIPMENT
Blunt-tipped yarn or tapestry needle, for weaving in yarn ends and sewing seams

GAUGES
2¼ fans of 7-dc measured over Fan Stitch Pattern, 6 trX sts measured over Hot Cross Bun Stitch Pattern, and 7 CL4 clusters measured over Cluster Stitch Pattern all to 4in (10cm) using a US size 7 (4.5mm) crochet hook. Each complete double dtr group of Zigzag Stitch Pattern measures 1⅜in (3.5cm) across using a US size 7 (4.5mm) crochet hook.

ABBREVIATIONS
See page 9.

SPECIAL ABBREVIATIONS
single dtr group = see page 62.
double dtr group = see page 62.
single end dtr group = see page 62.
trX (treble "X" shape—worked over 3 sts) = yo twice and insert hook in next stitch, yo and draw a loop through, yo and draw through first 2 loops on hook, skip next stitch, yo and insert hook in next stitch, yo and draw a loop through, [yo and draw through first 2 loops on hook] 4 times, ch 1, yo and insert hook halfway down stitch just made in place where lower "legs" join, yo and draw a loop through, [yo and draw through first 2 loops on hook] twice to complete trX.

3-dcCL (3-dc cluster) = [yo and insert hook in sp, yo and draw a loop through, yo and draw through first 2 loops on hook] 3 times in same sp (4 loops now on hook), yo and draw through all 4 loops on hook.

CL4 (cluster 4) = work 3 dc around stem of dc just worked but leaving last loop of each dc on hook, then work fourth dc where indicated leaving last loop of dc on hook as before (5 loops now on hook), yo and draw through all 5 loops on hook.

SIZES

To fit bust (inches)	30–32	34–36	38–40
To fit bust (cm)	76–81	86–91	97–102

FINISHED MEASUREMENTS

Around bust (inches)	35½	39	42½
Around bust (cm)	89	98	107
Length (inches)	21	22	22
Length (cm)	53	56	56
Sleeve seam (inches)	17¼	17¼	17¼
Sleeve seam (cm)	44	44	44

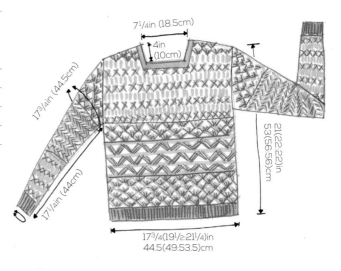

7¼in (18.5cm)
4in (10cm)
17¾in (44.5cm)
21(22:22)in 53(56:56)cm
17¼in (44cm)
17¾(19½:21¼)in 44.5(49:53.5)cm

BACK

Begin by working the rib, which is crocheted horizontally across body.

Foundation chain: Using a US size 7 (4.5mm) crochet hook, ch 15.

Cont working in rows, turning at end of each row.

Row 1 (RS): 1 sc in second ch from hook, 1 sc in each ch to end of row. *14 sc.*

Row 2: Ch 1 (does NOT count as a st), inserting hook under both loops of each sc, 1 sl st in each of next 14 sc.

Row 3: Ch 1 (does NOT count as a st), inserting hook under both loops of each sl st, 1 sc in each of next 14 sl sts.

[Rep Rows 2–3] 62(69:76) times more, do not turn at end of last row.

With RS facing, turn rib on its side, ch 1, then work 81(89:97) sc evenly across top of rib.

Fasten off.

FAN STITCH PATTERN

With RS facing, rejoin yarn with a sl st in first sc of rib. Cont working in rows, turning at end of each row.

Row 1 (RS): Ch 1, 1 sc in first sc (where sl st was worked), *skip 3 sc, 7 dc in next sc, skip 3 sc, 1 sc in next sc; rep from * to end of row. *10(11:12) 7-dc groups.*

Row 2: Ch 3 (counts as first dc), 1 dc in first sc, *ch 5, skip 7-dc group, work V-st of [1 dc, ch 1, 1 dc] in next sc; rep from * to last 7-dc group, ending with ch 5, skip last 7-dc group, 2 dc in last sc.

Row 3: Ch 3 (counts as first dc), 3 dc in first dc, *working over next 5-ch to enclose it, work 1 sc in fourth dc of 7-dc group in row below**, 7 dc in 1-ch sp at center of next V-st; rep from * ending last rep at **, 4 dc in top of tch.

Row 4: Ch 3, skip 4 dc, V-st in next sc, *ch 5, skip 7-dc group, V-st in next sc; rep from * ending ch 2, 1 sl st in top of tch.

Row 5: Ch 1, 1 sc in sl st, *7 dc in 1-ch sp at center of next V-st**, 1 sc in fourth dc of 7-dc group in row below; rep from * ending last rep at **, 1 sc in third of 3-ch at end.

Rep Rows 2–5 once more.

Rep Rows 2–3 once more.

Work final row of Fan Stitch Pattern as follows:

Next row (WS): Work as patt Row 4, but in place of 5-ch between V-sts work [ch 2, 1 sl st in fourth dc of 7-dc group, ch 2].

ZIGZAG STITCH PATTERN

Beg Zigzag Stitch Pattern as follows:

Row 1 (RS): Ch 1, 1 sc in each st to end of row, but decreasing 2(4:6) sts evenly across row. *79(85:91) sc.*

Row 2: Ch 1, 1 sc in each st to end of row.

Row 3: Ch 5 (counts as first dtr), skip first 3 sc, work 1 single dtr group in next sc, *1 double dtr group, ch 5; rep from * to last 3 sc, work 1 single end dtr group.

Row 4: Ch 1, 1 sc in top of first group, 5 sc in 5-ch sp, *1 sc in top of next group, 5 sc in next 5-ch sp; rep from * to last group, 1 sc in top of 5-ch at end of row.

Row 5: Ch 1, work 1 sc in each sc to end of row.

Rows 2–5 form the zigzag pattern.

Rep Rows 2–5 twice more.

Work Row 2 once more, but increasing 2(4:6) sts evenly across row. *81(89:97) sc.*

FAN STITCH PATTERN

Work Fan Stitch Pattern Rows 1–5.

HOT CROSS BUN STITCH PATTERN

Beg Hot Cross Bun Stitch Pattern as follows:

Row 1 (WS): Ch 1, 1 sc in each st, but increasing 2(3:1) sc evenly across row. *83(92:98) sc.*

Row 2: Ch 4 (counts as 1 tr), skip first sc, *trX over next 3 sc; rep from * ending 1 tr in last sc. *27(30:32) trXs.*

Row 3: Ch 4 (counts as 1 dc and 1-ch sp), *3-dcCL in next 1-ch sp**, ch 2; rep from * ending last rep at **, ch 1, 1 dc in top of tch. *27(30:32) 3-dcCLs.*

Row 4: Ch 1, 1 sc in first dc, 1 sc in next 1-ch sp, 1 sc in top of next cluster, *2 sc in next 2-ch sp, 1 sc in top of next cluster; rep from * ending with 1 sc in last sp (formed by 4-ch), 1 sc in third of 4-ch of previous row.***

Rep Rows 2–4 until work measures 8(9:9)in/ 20(22.5:22.5)cm from start of Hot Cross Bun Stitch Pattern, ending with a patt Row 4 (a sc row).

SHOULDER SHAPING

Row 1: Ch 1, sl st across first 12(15:18) sc, work as Row 2 of patt to last 12(15:18) sc, turn.

Row 3: Ch 1, sl st across first 12(15:15) sts, work as Row 3 of patt to last 12(15:15) sts, turn.

Row 4: Ch 1, 1 sc in each st.

Fasten off.

FRONT

Work as given for Back to ***.

Rep Rows 2–4 of Hot Cross Bun Stitch Pattern until Front measures 3in (7.5cm) less than Back to beginning of shoulder shaping, ending with a patt Row 4 (a sc row).

SHAPE NECK

Cont working in Hot Cross Bun Stitch Pattern, working each side of neck separately as follows:

Row 1: Work as patt Row 2 until there are 10(12:13) trXs, turn.

Row 2: Work as patt Row 3, turn.

Row 3: Work as patt Row 4, turn.

Row 4: Work as patt Row 5, decreasing one trX at neck edge.

Cont in Hot Cross Bun Stitch Pattern without shaping until Front has same number of rows as Back to shoulder shaping. Shape shoulder as for Back.

Fasten off.

Rejoin yarn to second side of neck and work in same way, reversing shaping.

SLEEVES (MAKE 2)

Foundation chain: Using a US size 7 (4.5mm) crochet hook, ch 57.

Cont working in rows, turning at end of each row.

HOT CROSS BUN STITCH PATTERN

Beg Hot Cross Bun Stitch Pattern as follows:

Row 1 (WS): Ch 1, 1 sc in second ch from hook, 1 sc in each ch to end of row. *56 sc.*

Row 2: Ch 4 (counts as 1 tr), skip first sc, *trX over next 3 sc; rep from * ending 1 tr in last sc. *Eighteen trXs.*

Row 3: Ch 4 (counts as 1 dc and 1-ch sp), *3-dcCL in next 1-ch sp**, ch 2; rep from * ending last rep at **, ch 1, 1 dc in top of tch. *Eighteen 3-dcCLs.*

Row 4: Ch 1, 1 sc in first dc, 1 sc in next 1-ch sp, 1 sc in top of next cluster, *2 sc in next 2-ch sp, 1 sc in top of next cluster; rep from * ending with 1 sc in last sp (formed by 4-ch), 1 sc in third of 4-ch of previous row.

Row 5: Ch 1, 1 sc in each sc.

Rep Rows 2–5 of Hot Cross Bun Stitch Pattern once more, increasing one 3-dcCL and one 2-ch sp at each end of patt Row 3. *62 sc.*

Rep Rows 2–5 of Hot Cross Bun Stitch Pattern once more without shaping.

Rep Rows 2–5 of Hot Cross Bun Stitch Pattern once more, increasing one 3-dcCL and one 2-ch sp at each end of patt Row 3. *68 sc.*

CLUSTER STITCH PATTERN

Beg Cluster Stitch Pattern as follows:

Row 1 (RS): Ch 3, skip first sc, work 1 dc in next sc, *ch 3, skip 1 sc, CL4 placing fourth dc of cluster in next sc, [ch 3, skip 2 sc, CL4 placing fourth dc of cluster in next sc] 3 times; rep from * to end. *24 CL4 clusters.*

Row 2: Ch 3, 1 dc in first 3-ch sp, *ch 3, CL4 placing fourth dc of cluster in next 3-ch space; rep from * to end, placing final dc of final cluster in top of 3-ch.

Row 3: Work as Row 2.

Row 4: Ch 3, 1 dc in first 3-ch sp, ch 3, CL4 placing fourth dc of cluster in same 3-ch sp (to increase one cluster), *ch 3, CL4 placing fourth dc in next 3-ch space; rep from * to end, increasing one cluster at end of row in same way. *26 CL4 clusters.*

Rep patt Rows 2–4 once more. *28 CL4 clusters.*

Rep patt Row 2 until Sleeve measures 11in (28cm), ending with a WS row.

Next row (RS): Ch 1, 2 sc in next 3-ch sp, *1 sc in top of next CL, 2 sc in next 3-ch sp; rep from * ending 1 sc in last dc. *84 sc.*

Next row: Ch 1, 1 sc in each sc, but decreasing 3 sts evenly across row. *81 sc.*

FAN STITCH PATTERN

Work Fan Stitch Pattern Rows 1–5, then rep patt Rows 2–5 until Sleeve measures 15in (38cm), ending with a patt Row 3.

Next row (WS): Work as patt Row 4, but in place of 5-ch between V-sts work [ch 2, 1 sl st in fourth dc of 7-dc group, ch 2].

Fasten off.

SLEEVE RIBS (MAKE 2)

The Sleeve ribs are worked separately as follows:

Foundation chain: Using a US size 7 (4.5mm) crochet hook, ch 15.

Rows 1–3: Work as for Rows 1–3 of Back rib.

[Rep Rows 2–3] 21(27:27) times more.

Fasten off.

Stretch each rib to fit along the bottom edge of the Sleeve and stitch in place.

TO FINISH

Weave in any yarn ends into the wrong side of the fabric so that they are not visible from the right side.

Sew together the Back and Front at the shoulders.

ADD NECK EDGING

With RS facing and using a US size 7 (4.5mm) crochet hook, join yarn to neck edge at left shoulder seam, ch 1, work sc evenly around neck edge, join with a sl st in top of first sc.

With RS always facing, work in rounds as follows:

Rounds 1–3: Ch 1, 1 sc in each st to end of round, join with a sl st in top of first sc.

Fasten off.

Mark positions of the tops of the Sleeves on the Back and Front, 8¾in (22cm) from shoulder seam. Pin the center of top of each Sleeve to shoulder seam and stitch the Sleeve in place between the markers.

Sew the side seams, stitching from the bottom edge of the garment up to the underarm, then down along the underarm Sleeve seams to the rib cuffs.

SHELL-EDGED CARDIGAN

//

YOU WILL NEED

YARN

Quince & Co. *Chickadee*, or a similar sport-weight wool yarn, in four colors:

A 7(8:8:8:9) x 50g (1¾oz) hanks in light blue (Bird's Egg)
B 1(1:1:1:1) x 50g (1¾oz) balls in pale yellow (Carrie's Yellow)
C 1(1:1:1:1) x 50g (1¾oz) balls in pale pink (Dogwood)
D 1(1:1:1:1) x 50g (1¾oz) balls in red (Pomegranate)

OTHER MATERIALS

Seven ⅞in (2cm) buttons

CROCHET HOOK

US size G/6 (4mm) crochet hook

OTHER EQUIPMENT

Blunt-tipped yarn or tapestry needle, for weaving in yarn ends and sewing seams

GAUGE

7½ V-sts and 10 rows to 4in (10cm) measured over V-st stitch pattern using a US size G/6 (4mm) crochet hook.

ABBREVIATIONS

See page 9.

SIZES

To fit bust (inches)	32	34	36	38	40
To fit bust (cm)	81	86	91	97	102

FINISHED MEASUREMENTS

Around bust (inches)	34¼	36¼	38½	40½	42½
Around bust (cm)	86.5	91	96.5	102.5	107
Length (inches)	20¾	21½	22	22¼	22¾
Length (cm)	52	54	55	56	57
Sleeve seam (inches), excluding cuff	16¾	17¼	17½	18	18
Sleeve seam (cm), excluding cuff	42	43	44	45	45

16¾(17¼:17½:18:18)in
42(43:44:45:45)cm

20¾(21½:22:22¼:22¾)in
52(54:55:56:57)cm

17(18:19¼:20¼:21¼)in
43(45.5:48:51:53.5)cm

BACK

Foundation chain: Using a US size G/6 (4mm) crochet hook and Col A, ch 97(103:109:115:121).

Cont working in rows, turning at end of each row.

Row 1 (RS): 1 dc in fourth ch from hook, *skip 2 ch, work a V-st of [1 dc, ch 1, 1 dc] in next ch; rep from * to last 3 ch, skip 2 ch, 1 dc in last ch.

Row 2: Ch 4, 1 dc in first dc, *V-st in second dc of next V-st; rep from * until 1 dc and tch rem, skip 1 dc and 1 ch, 1 dc in next ch.

Repeating Row 2 to form V-st patt, cont in V-st for 26(27:28:28:28) rows more using Col A.

Change to Col B and work one row in patt.

Change to Col A and work 2 rows in patt.

SHAPE ARMHOLE

Cut off yarn and fasten off, turn.

Cont working in stitch pattern as set, decreasing as follows:

Row 1: Rejoin Col A with a sl st in second dc of first(first:second:second:second) V-st, ch 4, 1 dc in same dc as sl st, *V-st in second dc of next V-st; rep from * until 1(1:2:2:2) full V-sts rem, 1 dc in second dc of next full V-st, turn. *Two(two:four:four:four) V-sts decreased.*

Row 2: Using Col C, ch 4, 1 dc in second dc of first V-st, *V-st in second dc of next V-st; rep from * to last full V-st, skip V-st and first ch of tch, 1 dc in next ch of tch. *Two V-sts decreased.*

Row 3: Using Col A, work as Row 2. *Two V-sts decreased.*

Bust sizes 32in (81cm), 34in (86cm), 36in (91cm), and 38in (97cm) only

Row 4: Using Col A, work in patt without shaping.

Bust size 40in (102cm) only

Row 4: Using Col A, work as Row 2. *Two V-sts decreased.*

All sizes

Rows 5 and 6: Using Col A, work in patt without shaping.

Row 7: Using Col D, work in patt without shaping. Change to Col A and work 12(13:13:14:15) rows more without shaping.

SHAPE SHOULDER

Cut off yarn and fasten off, turn.

Row 1: Skip first 2(3:3:3:3) V-sts and rejoin Col A with a sl st to second dc of next V-st, ch 3, *V-st in second dc of next V-st; rep from * until 3(4:4:4:5) V-sts rem, ch 3, 1 sc in second dc of next V-st.

Cut off yarn and fasten off, turn.

Row 2: Skip first 3(3:3:4:4) V-sts and rejoin Col A with a sl st to second dc of next V-st, ch 3, *V-st in second dc of next V-st; rep from * until 4(4:4:5:5) V-sts rem, ch 3, 1 sc in second dc of next V-st, turn.

Row 3: Ch 1, 1 sc in each dc and ch sp, 1 sc in top of tch. Fasten off.

FRONT (MAKE 2)

Foundation chain: Using a US size G/6 (4mm) crochet hook and Col A, ch 52(55:58:61:64).

Work as for Back to armhole shaping.

SHAPE ARMHOLE

Cont working in stitch pattern as set, decreasing as follows:

Row 1: Using Col A, work in patt until 1(1:2:2:2) full V-sts rem, 1 dc in second dc of next full V-st, turn. *One(one:two:two:two) V-sts decreased.*

Row 2: Using Col C, ch 4, 1 dc in second dc of first V-st, work in patt to end, turn. *One V-st decreased.*

Row 3: Using Col A, work in patt to last full V-st, skip V-st and first ch of tch, 1 dc in next ch of tch. *One V-st decreased.*

Bust sizes 32in (81cm), 34in (86cm), 36in (91cm), and 38in (97cm) only

Row 4: Using Col A, work in patt without shaping.

Bust size 40in (102cm) only

Row 4: Using Col A, work as Row 2. *One V-st decreased.*

All sizes

Rows 5 and 6: Using Col A, work in patt without shaping.

Row 7: Using Col D, work in patt without shaping. Change to Col A and work one more row in V-st patt without shaping, so ending at center front.

SHAPE NECKLINE

Cut off yarn and fasten off, turn.

Row 1: Skip first 3 V-sts and rejoin Col A with a sl st to second dc of next V-st, ch 3, *V-st in second dc of next V-st, work in patt to end of row, turn. *Four V-sts decreased.*

Row 2: Work in patt to last full V-st, skip V-st and first ch of tch, 1 dc in next ch of tch. *One V-st decreased.*
Row 3: Ch 4, 1 dc in second dc of first V-st, V-st in second dc of next V-st, work in patt to end of row, turn. *One V-st decreased.*
Work 8(9:9:10:11) rows in V-st patt without shaping.
Shape shoulder as for Back, but decreasing at sleeve edge only.
Fasten off.

SLEEVES (MAKE 2)
Foundation chain: Using a US size G/6 (4mm) crochet hook and Col A, ch 49(49:49:52:52).
Cont working in rows, turning at end of each row.
Row 1 (RS): 1 dc in fourth ch from hook, *skip 2 ch, work a V-st of [1 dc, ch 1, 1 dc] in next ch; rep from * to last 3 ch, skip 2 ch, 1 dc in last ch.
Row 2: Ch 4, 1 dc in first dc, *V-st in second dc of next V-st; rep from * until 1 dc and tch rem, skip 1 dc and 1 ch, 1 dc in next ch.
SHAPE SLEEVE
Cont repeating Row 2 to form patt and at the same time inc 1 V-st in 3rd row, then every 5th(5th:4th:4th:3rd) row 3(3:9:9:3) times more, then every 4th row 5(5:0:0:7) times more, working each inc row as follows:
Inc row: Work in patt as set to V-st at center of row, then work one V-st of each dc of center V-st, cont in patt to end of row. *One V-st increased.*
After all incs have been completed, cont without shaping until 42(43:44:45:45) rows have been worked from foundation-chain edge.
SHAPE SLEEVE CAP
Cut off yarn and fasten off, turn.
Cont working in stitch pattern as set, decreasing as follows:
Row 1: Rejoin Col A with a sl st in second dc of first(first:first:second:second) V-st, ch 4, 1 dc in same dc as sl st, *V-st in second dc of next V-st; rep from * until 1(1:1:2:2) full V-sts rem, 1 dc in second dc of next full V-st, turn. *Two(two:two:four:four) V-sts decreased.*
**Work one row in patt without shaping.
Dec row: Ch 4, 1 dc in second dc of first V-st, *V-st in second dc of next V-st; rep from * to last full V-st, skip V-st and first ch of tch, 1 dc in next ch of tch. *Two V-sts decreased.**

Rep from ** to ** once more.
Work 4(5:5:6:6) rows in patt without shaping.
Dec 2 V-sts as before on next row and then every alt row twice, then on every row twice more.
Next row: Ch 1, 1 sc in each st and ch sp to end of row.
Fasten off.

TO FINISH
Weave in any yarn ends into the wrong side of the fabric so that they are not visible from the right side.
Sew together the Back and Fronts at the shoulders.
Pin the Sleeve caps into the armholes to keep them in position while sewing. Sew Sleeve caps in place.
Sew the Back and Fronts together along the side seams, stitching from the bottom edge of the garment up to the underarm, then down along the underarm Sleeve seams.
ADD COLLAR
With RS facing and using a US size G/6 (4mm) crochet hook, join Col A to beg of neck edge at the center Front and work Collar in rows, turning at end of each row, as follows:
Row 1 (RS): Ch 1, work sc evenly around neckline, turn.
Row 2: Ch 2, then working in back loop only, 1 hdc in each of next 5 sts, 2 hdc in next st, *1 hdc in each of next 6 sts, 2 hdc in next st; rep from * to end of row, ending with 1 hdc into any rem sts that repeat doesn't fit into.
Row 3: Ch 2, 1 hdc in each of next 6 sts (working through both loops in the usual way from this row on), 2 hdc in next st, *1 hdc in each of next 7 sts, 2 hdc in next st; rep from * to end of row, ending with 1 hdc into any rem sts that repeat doesn't fit into.
Row 4: Using Col D, ch 2, 1 hdc in each of next 7 sts, 2 hdc in next st, *1 hdc in each of next 8 sts, 2 hdc in next st; rep from * to end of row, ending with 1 hdc into any rem sts that repeat doesn't fit into.
Row 5: Using Col A, ch 2, *1 hdc in next st; rep from * to end of row.
Row 6: Using Col C, ch 2, 1 hdc in each of next 9 sts, 2 hdc in next st, *1 hdc in each of next 10 sts, 2 hdc in next st; rep from * to end of row, ending with 1 hdc into any rem sts that repeat doesn't fit into.
Row 7: Using Col A, ch 2, *1 hdc in next st; rep from * to end of row.

Row 8: Using Col B, ch 2, 1 hdc in each of next 12 sts, 2 hdc in next st, *1 hdc in each of next 13 sts, 2 hdc in next st; rep from * to end of row, ending with 1 hdc into any rem sts that repeat doesn't fit into.

At end of last row count your collar sts and make sure you have a multiple of 4 sts plus one st extra so you can work the shell st patt evenly along Row 9; if you don't have the correct number of sts, undo the row and add the number of extra sts you need evenly across the row to obtain the correct multiple while also increasing at the intervals required in Row 8.

Row 9 (shell st patt): Using Col A, ch 1, 1 sc in first st, *skip 1 st, 5 dc in next st, skip 1 st, 1 sc in next st; rep from * to end of row.

Fasten off.

ADD CUFFS

With RS facing and using a US size G/6 (4mm) crochet hook, join Col D to the edge at Sleeve seam and add a cuff in rounds around bottom of each Sleeve with RS always facing as follows:

Round 1 (RS): Ch 2, 1 hdc in each of next 3 sts, 2 hdc in next st, *1 hdc in each of next 4 sts, 2 hdc in next st; rep from * to end of round, join with a sl st in top of 2-ch.

Round 2: Using Col C, ch 3, 1 dc in each of next 4 sts, 2 dc in next st, *1 dc in each of next 5 sts, 2 dc in next st; rep from * to end of round, join with a sl st in top of 3-ch.

Round 3: Using Col B, ch 3, 1 dc in each of next 5 sts, 2 dc in next st, *1 dc in each of next 6 sts, 2 dc in next st; rep from * to end of round, join with a sl st in top of 3-ch.

At end of last round count your cuff sts and make sure you have a multiple of 4 sts (counting the 3-ch as one st) so you can work the shell st patt evenly along Round 4; if you don't have the correct number of sts, undo the round and add the number of extra sts you need evenly across the round to obtain the correct multiple while also increasing at the intervals required in Round 3.

Round 4 (shell st patt): Using Col A, ch 1, 1 sc in top of 3-ch, skip 1 st, 5 dc in next st, skip 1 st, *1 sc in next st, skip 1 st, 5 dc in next st, skip 1 st; rep from * to end of round, join with a sl st in top of first sc.

Fasten off.

ADD EDGING ALONG BOTTOM OF CARDIGAN

With RS facing and using a US size G/6 (4mm) crochet hook, join Col D to the edge at center front of Left Front and work edging along bottom of cardigan as follows:

Row 1 (RS): Ch 3, work dc evenly along bottom of cardigan to center front of Right Front, turn.

Row 2: Ch 3, 1 dc in each st to end of row.

Fasten off.

ADD BUTTON BAND

With RS facing and using a US size G/6 (4mm) crochet hook, join Col B to top of center edge of Left Front and work button band on Left Front as follows:

Row 1 (RS): Ch 3, work dc evenly all the way down Front and across bottom edging, turn.

Row 2: Ch 1, 1 sc in each st to end of row, turn.

Row 3: Ch 3, 1 dc in each st to end of row.

Fasten off.

ADD BUTTONHOLE BAND

Mark the positions for the seven buttons along the button band. Place markers on the Right Front at the position of each button so you can work your buttonholes to match the button positions.

With right side facing and using a US size G/6 (4mm) crochet hook, join Col B to bottom of center edge of Right Front and work buttonhole band as follows:

Row 1 (RS): Ch 3, dc evenly all the way up front to top edge, turn.

Row 2: Ch 1, *1 sc in each st until next buttonhole position, ch 2, skip 2 sts; rep from * until last buttonhole has been worked, 1 sc in each st to end of row, turn.

Row 3: Ch 3, 1 dc in each st to end of row.

Fasten off.

Sew buttons on Left Front button band to match buttonholes on Right Front.

KIMONO JACKET

YOU WILL NEED

YARN

Jamieson's of Shetland *DK* or a similar sport-weight yarn in five colors:

A 9(10:11) x 25g (⅞oz) balls in purple-blue (629 Lupin)
B 8(9:10) x 25g (⅞oz) balls in bright pink (585 Plum)
C 2(2:3) x 25g (⅞oz) balls in pale blue (655 China Blue)
D 2(2:3) x 25g (⅞oz) balls in yellow (400 Mimosa)
E 3(3:4) x 25g (⅞oz) balls in light orange (308 Tangerine)

CROCHET HOOK

US size G/6 (4mm) crochet hook

OTHER EQUIPMENT

Blunt-tipped yarn or tapestry needle, for weaving in yarn ends and sewing seams

GAUGE

17 stitches and 12 rows to 4in (10cm) measured over spike stitch pattern using a US size G/6 (4mm) hook.

ABBREVIATIONS

See page 9.

SIZES

To fit bust (inches)	32–34	36–38	40
To fit bust (cm)	81–86	91–97	102

FINISHED MEASUREMENTS

Around bust (inches)	43	45¾	48¾
Around bust (cm)	108	114.5	122
Length (inches)	19¼	20	20½
Length (cm)	49	51	53
Sleeve seam (inches)	8	8	8½
Sleeve seam (cm)	20	20	21

SPIKE STITCH

Step 1 Work up to the point where you would like to make the spike stitch. Yo and insert your hook into the space created in the row or rows below.

Step 2 Yo and draw through a long loop, feeding your hook with slightly more yarn than usual so your work does not pucker. Finish working your double as usual.

Step 3 Work to the end of your row and you will see your double-crochet spike stitches extending down into the row below.

+ BOBBLE STITCH

STEP 1 The bobbles are worked with the wrong side facing you but they appear on the right side. Begin your stitch with yo, then insert the hook into the next stitch.

STEP 2 Yo and draw a loop through the stitch.

STEP 3 Yo and draw a loop through the first two loops sitting on your hook. Do not finish this stitch off.

STEP 4 Repeat steps 1–3, but working into the same stitch. You will now have three loops sitting on your hook.

STEP 5 Repeat steps 1–3 until you have worked five stitches into the same stitch. You should now have six loops in total sitting on your crochet hook.

STEP 6 Yo and draw a loop through all six loops on the hook, pushing the bobble to the right side of the work.

STEP 7 The single crochet worked in the next stitch along fastens your bobble in place on the right side of the crochet fabric.

STEP 8 Work to the end of the row. Turn the work over and you will see all your lovely bobbles on the right side of your work.

BACK

Foundation chain: Using a US size G/6 (4mm) crochet hook and Col E, ch 92(98:104).

BOBBLE STITCH PATTERN

Cont working in rows, turning at end of each row.

Row 1 (RS): 1 sc in third ch from hook (counts as first 2 sts), 1 sc in each ch to end of row. *91(97:103) sts.*

Row 2: Ch 2 (counts as first sc), skip first sc, *work bobble st (see left) in next sc, 1 sc in next sc; rep from * to end of row, working last sc of last rep in top of tch.

Row 3: Change to Col A, ch 2 (counts as first sc), skip first sc, 1 sc in each st to end of row, working last sc in top of tch.

Row 4: Work as Row 3.

Rows 5–6: Change to Col B, work as Row 3.

Rows 7–8: Change to Col A, work as Row 3.

Row 9: Change to Col D, work as Row 3.

Row 10: Ch 2 (counts as first sc), skip first sc, *work bobble st in next sc, 1 sc in next sc; rep from * to end of row, working last sc of last rep in top of tch.

Rows 11–16: Work as Rows 3–8.

Rows 17–18: Change to Col C, work as Rows 9–10, but decreasing one st at end of last row by omitting last sc. *90(96:102) sts.*

SPIKE STITCH PATTERN

Begin pattern as follows:

Row 1 (RS): Change to Col A, ch 3 (counts as first dc), skip first st, 1 dc in each of next 2 sts, *ch 1, 1 dc in each of next 3 sts; rep from * to end of row, working last dc of last rep in top of tch.

Row 2: Ch 3 (counts as first dc), skip first dc, 1 dc in each of next 2 dc, *skip 1-ch sp, 1 dc in each of next 3 dc; rep from * to end of row, working last dc of last rep in top of tch.

Row 3: Change to Col B, ch 3 (counts as first dc), skip first 2 dc, *1 dc in next dc, work 1 double-crochet spike st (see page 134) in sp between sts 2 rows below, 1 dc in next dc, skip 1 dc; rep from * to end of row, ending with 1 dc in top of tch.

Row 4: Ch 3 (counts as first dc), skip first dc, *1 dc in next dc; rep from * to end of row, ending with 1 dc in top of tch.

Row 5: Change to Col A, ch 3 (counts as first dc), skip first dc, 1 spike st in sp between sts 2 rows below, 1 dc in next dc, *skip 1 dc, 1 dc in next dc, 1 spike st in sp between sts 2 rows below, 1 dc in next dc; rep from * to end of row, working last dc of last rep in top of tch.

Row 6: Work as Row 4.

Rows 3–6 form the Spike Stitch Pattern. Cont working in this patt until work measures 10(10½:10½)in/25(26:26)cm from foundation-ch edge, ending with a WS row.

SHAPE RAGLAN

Cont working in Spike Stitch Pattern, but at the same time work decs by skipping sts as follows:

Dec row 1 (RS): Ch 3, skip 1 st, work in patt as set to last 2 sts, skip 1 st, 1 dc in last st. *Two sts decreased.*

Dec row 2: Ch 3, skip 2 sts, work in patt as set to last 3 sts, skip 2 sts, 1 dc in last st. *Four sts decreased.*

Rep these 2 dec rows 10(11:12) times more, then rep Dec Row 1 once(once:–) more so that 22(22:24) sts rem. Work 1(1:0) rows more in patt without shaping. Fasten off.

LEFT FRONT

Foundation chain: Using a US size G/6 (4mm) crochet hook and Col E, ch 46(50:52).

BOBBLE STITCH PATTERN

Cont working in rows, turning at end of each row.

Row 1 (RS): 1 sc in third ch from hook (counts as first 2 sts), 1 sc in each ch to end of row. *45(49:51) sts.*

Work as Rows 2–16 of Bobble Stitch as for Back, then complete border as follows:

Rows 17–18: Change to Col C, work as patt Rows 9–10, but decreasing 0(1:0) st at end of last row by omitting last sc. *45(48:51) sts.*

Work Spike Stitch Pattern for same number of rows as Back until raglan shaping, so ending with a WS row.**

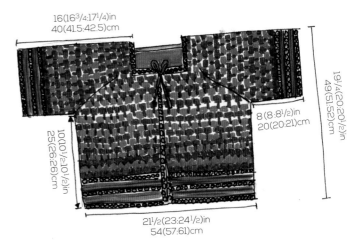

16(16¾:17¼)in
40(41.5:42.5)cm

19¼(20:20½)in
49(51:52)cm

8(8:8½)in
20(20:21)cm

10(10½:10½)in
25(26:26)cm

21½(23:24½)in
54(57:61)cm

SHAPE RAGLAN

Cont working in Spike Stitch Pattern, but at the same time work decs by skipping sts as follows:

Dec row 1 (RS): Ch 3, skip 1 st, work in patt to end of row. *One st decreased.*

Dec row 2: Work in patt to last 3 sts, skip 2 sts, 1 dc in last st. *Two sts decreased.*

Rep these 2 dec rows 9(9:10) times more, then rep Dec Row 1 –(once:–) more so that 15(17:18) sts rem. Work 0(1:0) rows more in patt without shaping. Fasten off.

RIGHT FRONT

Work as for Left Front to **.

SHAPE RAGLAN

Cont working in Spike Stitch Pattern, but at the same time work decs by skipping sts as follows:

Dec row 1 (RS): Work in patt as set to last 2 sts, skip 1 st, 1 dc in last st. *One st decreased.*

Dec row 2: Ch 3, skip 2 sts, work in patt as set to end of row. *Two sts decreased.*

Rep these 2 dec rows 9(9:10) times more, then rep Dec Row 1 –(once:–) more so that 15(17:18) sts rem. Work 0(1:0) rows more in patt without shaping. Fasten off.

SLEEVES (MAKE 2)

Foundation chain: Using a US size G/6 (4mm) crochet hook and Col E, ch 86(88:92).

BOBBLE STITCH PATTERN

Cont working in rows, turning at end of each row.

Row 1 (RS): 1 sc in third ch from hook (counts as first 2 sts), 1 sc in each ch to end of row. *85(87:91) sts.*

Work as Rows 2–16 of Bobble Stitch for Back, then complete border as follows:

Rows 17–18: Change to Col C, work as patt Rows 9–10, but decreasing 1(0:1) st at end of last row by omitting last sc. *84(87:90) sts.*

Work Spike Stitch Pattern as for Back until work measures (8(8:8½)in/20(20:21)cm, ending at the same point in the patt rep as on Back and Fronts at beg of raglan shaping and so ending with a WS row.

SHAPE RAGLAN

Cont working in spike stitch pattern, but at the same time rep Dec Rows 1 and 2 of Back 10(11:11) times so that 24(21:24) sts rem and raglan is 4 rows shorter than Back to neck edge.

Left sleeve only

Row 1: Ch 3, skip 1 st, work in patt to end of row. *One st decreased.*

Row 2: Work to last 3 sts, skip 2 sts, 1 dc in last st. *Two sts decreased.*

Row 3: Work as Row 1.

Row 4: Work to last 3 sts, skip 0(0:2) sts, 1 dc in last st. *20(17:18) sts.*

Fasten off.

Right sleeve only

Work as for last 4 rows of Left Sleeve but reversing shaping.

TO FINISH

Weave in any yarn ends to the wrong side of your work so they are not visible on the right side.

Matching the stripes, sew together the raglan edges of the Left Front and Left Sleeve, joining the straight edge of the last 4 rows at the top of the Left Sleeve to the top edge of the Left Front. Sew the Right Front to the Right Sleeve in the same way. Then sew together the raglan edges of the Back and the Sleeves.

Finally, sew up the side seams, stitching upward from the bottom of the garment all the way up to the underarm and then down along the Sleeve seam.

ADD FRONT EDGING

With RS facing and using a US size G/6 (4mm) crochet hook, join Col E to the beginning of the center front edge of the Left Front, ch 2 (counts as first sc), then work an even number of sc all along the edge, turn.

Work Row 2 of the Bobble Stitch Pattern as for the Back. Fasten off.

Repeat along the center front edge of the Right Front.

ADD NECKLINE EDGING

With RS facing and using a US size G/6 (4mm) crochet hook, join Col E to the beginning of the neck edge on the Right Front, ch 2 (counts as first sc), then work an even number of sc all along the neck edge until you reach the center front of the Left Front, turn.

Work Row 2 of the Bobble Stitch Pattern as for the Back. Fasten off.

TIES (MAKE 2)

Using a US size G/6 (4mm) crochet hook and Col E, ch 61.

Row 1: 1 sc in second ch from hook, *1 sc in each ch to end of row, turn.

Row 2: Ch 2 (counts as first sc), skip first sc, *1 sc in next sc; rep from * to end of row.

Fasten off.

Sew one tie to the neckline edging of both the Left and Right Fronts on the wrong side of the fabric.

⊹YARN INFORMATION

The specifications of all the yarns used in this book are given here. If you want to use a substitute yarn, choose one that has the same recommended needle size and knitting gauge over stockinette stitch (St st) as the specified yarn.

BC GARN SEMILLA
100% organic wool; 175yd (160m) per 50g (1¾oz) ball; recommended gauge 22 sts and 30 rows to 4in (10cm) measured over St st using US size 6 (4mm) knitting needles; *http://garn.dk*

BC GARN SEMILLA GROSSO
100% organic wool; 87½yd (80m) per 50g (1¾oz) ball; recommended gauge 15 sts and 20 rows to 4in (10cm) measured over St st using US size 10 (6mm) knitting needles; *http://garn.dk*

DEBBIE BLISS RIALTO DK
100% merino wool; 115yd (105m) per 50g (1¾oz) ball; recommended gauge 22 sts and 30 rows to 4in (10cm) measured over St st using US size 6 (4mm) knitting needles; *http://debbieblissonline.com*

DROPS ALPACA 4PLY
100% alpaca; 182½yd (167m) per 50g (1¾oz) ball; recommended gauge 23 sts and 30 rows to 4in (10cm) measured over St st using US size 2–4 (2.5–3.5mm) knitting needles; *http://garnstudio.com*

GINGER'S HAND DYED SHEEPISH DK
100% wool; 246yd (225m) per 100g (3½oz) hank; recommended gauge 22 sts and 28 rows to 4in (10cm) measured over St st using US size 6 (4mm) knitting needles; *http://www.gingertwiststudios.com*

JAMIESON'S OF SHETLAND DK
100% wool; 82yd (75m) per 25g (⅞ oz) ball; recommended gauge 25 sts and 32 rows to 4in (10cm) measured over St st using US size 5 (3.75mm) knitting needles; *http://www.jamiesonsofshetland.co.uk*

JAMIESON'S OF SHETLAND SPINDRIFT
100% wool; 115yd (105m) per 25g (⅞oz) ball; recommended gauge 30 sts and 32 rows to 4in (10cm) measured over St st using US size 3 (3.25mm) knitting needles; *http://www.jamiesonsofshetland.co.uk*

JC RENNIE SUPERSOFT LAMBSWOOL 4PLY
100% wool; 269yd (246m) per 50g (1¾oz) ball; recommended gauge 28 sts and 36 rows to 4in (10cm) measured over St st using US size 3 (3mm) knitting needles; *http://www.knitrennie.com*

JILL DRAPER MAKES STUFF HUDSON
100% merino wool; 240yd (219m) per 113g (4oz) hank; recommended gauge 16–20 sts to 4in (10cm) measured over St st using US size 7–8 (4.5–5mm) knitting needles; *https://www.etsy.com/uk/shop/jilldrapermakesstuff*

MISTI ALPACA CHUNKY
100% alpaca; 109yd (100m) per 100g (3½oz) ball; recommended gauge 14 sts to 4in (10cm) measured over St st using US size 10 (6mm) knitting needles; *http://mistialpaca.com*

ORKNEY ANGORA ST MAGNUS DK
50% angora, 50% wool; 218yd (200m) per 50g (1¾oz) ball; recommended gauge 20 sts to 4in (10cm) measured over St st using US size 4 (3.5mm) knitting needles; *http://orkneyangora.co.uk*

PRICK YOUR FINGER CARPET YARN
100% wool; 100g (3½oz) ball; recommended needles US size 7 (4.5mm); *http://prickyourfinger.com*

QUINCE & CO. CHICKADEE
100% wool; 181yd (166m) per 50g (1¾oz) hank; recommended gauge 26 sts to 4in (10cm) measured over St st using US size 3 (3.25mm) knitting needles; *http://quinceandco.com*

QUINCE & CO. OSPREY
100% wool; 170yd (155m) per 100g (3½oz) hank; recommended gauge 16 sts to 4in (10cm) measured over St st using US size 9 (5.5mm) knitting needles; *http://quinceandco.com*

RICO FASHION COLOUR TOUCH
98% wool, 2% polyester; 98yd (90m) per 100g (3½oz) ball; recommended gauge 12 sts and 16 rows to 4in (10cm) measured over St st using US size 13 (9mm) knitting needles; *http://www.rico-design.de*

RICO CREATIVE COTTON ARAN
100% cotton; 93yd (85m) per 50g (1¾oz) ball; recommended gauge 18 sts and 24 rows to 4in (10cm) measured over St st using US size 6–8 (4–5mm) knitting needles; *http://www.rico-design.de*

RICO ESSENTIALS COTTON DK
100% cotton; 142yd (130m) per 50g (1¾oz) ball; recommended gauge 22 sts and 28 rows to 4in (10cm) measured over St st using US size 6 (4mm) knitting needles; *http://www.rico-design.de*

ROWAN HANDKNIT COTTON
100% cotton; 93yd (85m) per 50g (1¾oz) ball; recommended gauge 19–20 sts and 28 rows to 4in (10cm) measured over St st using US size 6–7 (4–4.5mm) knitting needles; *http://www.knitrowan.com*

ROWAN ORIGINAL DENIM
100% cotton; 100yd (92m) per 50g (1¾oz) ball; recommended gauge 20 sts and 32 rows to 4in (10cm) measured over St st using US size 6 (4mm) knitting needles; *http://www.knitrowan.com*

ROWAN PURE WOOL 4PLY
100% wool; 174yd (160m) per 50g (1¾oz) ball; recommended gauge 28 sts and 36 rows to 4in (10cm) measured over St st using US size 3 (3.25mm) knitting needles; *http://www.knitrowan.com*

ROWAN MOHAIR HAZE
30% wool, 70% mohair; 112yd (102m) per 25g (⅞ oz) ball; recommended gauge 28 sts and 36 rows to 4in (10cm) measured over St st using US size 2–3 (3mm) knitting needles; *http://www.knitrowan.com*

WOOL AND THE GANG SHINY HAPPY COTTON
100% cotton; 155yd (142m) per 100g (3½oz) ball; recommended gauge 16 sts to 4in (10cm) measured over St st using US size 8 (5mm) knitting needles; *http://www.woolandthegang.com*

YEOMAN YARNS CANNELLE 4PLY
100% cotton; 929½yd (850m) per 245g (8½ oz) cone; recommended gauge 33 sts and 44 rows to 4in (10cm) measured over St st using US size 2 (2.75mm) knitting needles; *http://yeoman-yarns.co.uk*

MEET THE TEAM

PUBLISHING DIRECTOR Jane O'Shea
COMMISSIONING EDITOR Lisa Pendreigh
EDITORIAL ASSISTANT Harriet Butt
PATTERN CHECKER Luise Roberts
CREATIVE DIRECTOR Helen Lewis
ART DIRECTION AND DESIGN Claire Peters
PRODUCTION DIRECTOR Vincent Smith
PRODUCTION CONTROLLER Tom Moore

PHOTOGRAPHER Laura Edwards
PHOTOGRAPHER'S ASSISTANTS Alex
Davenport, Suzie Howell & Kim Lightbody
STYLIST Verity Pemberton
HAIR AND MAKE-UP ARTISTS Terri Capon
& Danni Hooker
MODELS Rebecca Arnold at Nevs, Claudia
Devlin at Nevs, Emily Green at M&P and
Drew Gregory Fountain at FM
HAND MODEL Chinh Hoang

First published in 2015 by Quadrille Publishing Ltd.
Pentagon House
52–54 Southwark Street
London SE1 1UN
www.quadrille.com

Quadrille
craft

www.quadrillecraft.com

Quadrille is an imprint of Hardie Grant
www.hardiegrant.com.au

Text, projects and designs
© 2015 Anna Wilkinson
Photography
© 2015 Laura Edwards
Artwork, design and layout
© 2015 Quadrille Publishing Ltd.

British Library Cataloguing-In-Publication Data
A catalogue record for this book is available from the British Library.

ISBN 978 184949 7534

10 9 8 7 6 5 4 3 2 1

Printed in China.

If you have any comments
or queries regarding the
instructions in this book,
please contact us at
enquiries@quadrille.co.uk.

I would like to say a huge thank you to everyone at Quadrille for all their hard work and for making such a lovely book that I feel incredibly proud to have my name on the front of. Thank you to Lisa for giving me the opportunity to write this book and to Claire for making it look so lovely. I know there are so many people who have worked on this book and made it what it is, so thank you so much to you all. To Laura, Verity and everyone who was involved in the photoshoots—thank you for getting such beautiful photographs and for making the days fun. I couldn't be happier with this book and I'm so lucky to have had such amazing and creative people work on it.

Thank you to all the crocheters, Victoria Stott, Joanna Wilkinson, Helen Barber, and Camilla Fraser, who helped me to create all the projects in this book and for being so reliable and hard working. A huge thank you also to the lovely Jess from Ginger Twist Studio for the gorgeous pink yarn used for the Patchwork Stitch Jumper.

My biggest thank you goes to Richard and to my lovely parents, Joanna and Martin, for their continuous, unending encouragement and support in whatever I set my mind to.